Getting Started With OpenShift

T0385757

Steven Pousty and Katie J. Miller

Beijing · Cambridge · Farnham · Köln · Sebastopol · Tokyo

Getting Started With OpenShift

by Steven Pousty and Katie J. Miller

Printed in the United States of America.

Published by O'Reilly Media, Inc., 1005 Gravenstein Highway North, Sebastopol, CA 95472.

O'Reilly books may be purchased for educational, business, or sales promotional use. Online editions are also available for most titles (*http://my.safaribooksonline.com*). For more information, contact our corporate/institutional sales department: 800-998-9938 or *corporate@oreilly.com*.

Editor: Brian Anderson
Production Editor: Melanie Yarbrough
Copyeditor: Charles Roumeliotis
Proofreader: Rachel Head

Cover Designer: Karen Montgomery
Interior Designer: David Futato
Illustrator: Rebecca Demarest

March 2014:   First Edition

Revision History for the First Edition:

2014-03-26:   First release

See *http://oreilly.com/catalog/errata.csp?isbn=9781491901434* for release details.

ISBN: 978-1-491-90143-4

[LSI]

Table of Contents

Preface

One of the newest and most promising trends in application development and DevOps is the rise of Platform as a Service (PaaS). If you haven't heard of it yet, you will learn more in Chapter 1. Trust us for now when we say it promises to greatly simplify application development and system administration work for web applications. It is also one of the few new technologies that actually helps developers and sys admins to get along, allowing each to trust/enable the other and be happy that their needs are being met. This book is focused on giving the application developer a quick yet ample introduction to Red Hat's PaaS, OpenShift.

Fundamentally, the reason you want to use OpenShift is because you like writing applications, not administering servers. With just a couple of changes to the way you develop applications, you can spin up your web server and database with one command. You will no longer need to keep a server operating system up-to-date, patch the web servers, maintain the DNS, and do all the other tasks that distract you from writing code. By the end of reading this guide you will be all set to build, deploy, and host your applications on OpenShift.

Who Should Read This Book

First and foremost, those who are impatient! You don't want to sit down and read a lengthy "Authoritative Guide" or a "Reference Manual." You want a nice succinct book to get you going on OpenShift as quickly as possible. If you like the platform and can successfully develop an initial application for it, *then* you will sit down and read more thorough guides. Given this goal, we do not delve very deeply into any particular topic and there are specific topics we leave out, such as how you build custom server plugins to run on OpenShift.

You are a web or mobile application developer—you write apps that use HTTP for part or all of their communication with end users. Perhaps you hate doing sys admin work; this is perfect because deploying your application on a Platform as a Service allows you to bypass what we consider drudgery. If you are a system adminstrator and you want to learn more about providing OpenShift as a development platform, have a look at the Administration Guide (*http://openshift.github.io/documentation/oo_administra tion_guide.html*).

As the title indicates, we are assuming little in the way of background knowledge except:

- You know how to create a web application.
- You know how to use the command line.
- You can program in one of the six main programming languages OpenShift supports.
- You can use a text editor on a console; the most basic is Nano (*http://www.nano-editor.org/docs.php*) but Vim or Emacs will be OK as well.

We also assume some familiarity with basic Linux commands. If you have not used a Unix-like terminal, we recommend you review Appendix A.

This guide is intended for programmers who want to get started using OpenShift as quickly as possible, but also want to understand a little bit of what they are doing.

Why We Wrote This Book

We want to enable you to become self-sufficient in the basic use of OpenShift for creating and hosting your web applications, in as few words as possible. Therefore, we will not go into long explanations of the technologies used in OpenShift or different programming paradigms, but instead will give you links where you can go to read more.

This book grew out of the numerous workshops and talks we have given for developers. Unfortunately, we cannot be in all the places we want to be or talk to all the developers we want to meet. Our hope is for the book to help scale out our ability to teach more people the joy of developing on OpenShift.

Introducing the Insult Application

In the course of this book we are going to build a very simple but devastatingly effective application—a Shakespearean insult generator. It will combine two random adjectives and a noun to insult the user of the web page. It can be found online, running on OpenShift (*http://insultapp-osbeginnerbook.rhcloud.com/*). The app will evolve as we go through the book; it will start as a simple *Hello World* application, and we will add features until finally it will pull the adjectives and nouns out of a database. We will use the application's development as a means of introducing you to the different aspects of creating and maintaining an application on OpenShift.

For the purposes of this book, we wrote the code in Python, at the risk of alienating programmers who use other supported languages. Hear us out while we explain our reasoning on why Python was the best choice. The book needed to be short, so we did not have room to put code samples for all of OpenShift's supported languages in the text itself. Python is one of the top three programming languages used on OpenShift. We believe that Python is a very readable language (if you can get over your fear of indentation), even to those who are not yet familiar with its syntax. We have endeavored to keep the code base simple; developers of all kinds should be able to follow the code examples.

The goal of this book was *not* to make you a better Python programmer. It does not go into Python best practices, it does not use a lot of the more advanced libraries, and it does not show advanced usage of Python on OpenShift. For example, it is possible to use *app.py* in your application to specify a web server other than Apache with *mod_wsgi*. We do not cover those topics here because the application is merely a vehicle to introduce OpenShift's functionality, which is language agnostic. We plan to post ports of the application to other languages on the GitHub site for the book. Please check there or help us by porting yourself—we love pull requests.

How This Book Is Organized

The aim of this book is to get you up and running on OpenShift as quickly as possible. To that end, we dive into the most crucial content first and fill in the finer details as we go along.

Chapter 1 defines Platform as a Service and OpenShift, and gives an overview of the basic terms, technologies, and commands you will need to understand for the rest of the book.

Chapter 2 through Chapter 4 demonstrate how to create and modify OpenShift applications with a variety of components and capabilities. By the end of Chapter 4, you will know how to create your own OpenShift application with support for a given programming language, database, and/or other technologies.

Chapter 5 and Chapter 6 explain some of the key application management mechanisms and how to connect your application code with your OpenShift database.

Chapter 7 through Chapter 9 delve into details you may need to support your particular application's needs, such as the use of certain ports or persistent storage space, and to maintain your app in the long term.

Chapter 10 outlines the platform's support for team development work.

Chapter 11 summarizes the book and presents some additional resources for those interested in more detail on OpenShift.

Online Resources

As you read through this book, you can try out what you are learning by signing up for a free account at OpenShift.com (*http://www.openshift.com*). The code examples shown, as well as additional resources, are available on GitHub (see "Using Code Examples" on page xi for more information).

Throughout the text we use the command line to interact with OpenShift, utilizing the Red Hat Cloud (RHC) client tools. This is a fast and convenient way to interact with OpenShift that will be familiar to many developers; however, there are other options for those who prefer a graphical approach. You can find more information about the OpenShift Web Console (*https://www.openshift.com/get-started#web*) and read about OpenShift plug-ins (*https://www.openshift.com/get-started#ide*) for integrated development environments (IDEs)on the OpenShift website.

This book aims to provide the key information a developer needs to get started with OpenShift; we do not show every possible command or option. If you would like more details, please see the documentation and other resources at the OpenShift Developer Center (*https://www.openshift.com/developers*).

If you would like to write your own cartridges for OpenShift, you will want to check out the Cartridge Developer's Guide (*http://openshift.github.io/documentation/oo_cartridge_developers_guide.html*); we do not cover this topic.

A huge range of programming languages, frameworks, and technologies can run on OpenShift; to find out more about support for your favorites and the latest platform developments, we recommend reading the OpenShift blog (*http://blog.openshift.com*).

If you have questions or issues, you can reach the OpenShift team through Stack Overflow (*http://stackoverflow.com/questions/tagged/openshift*), via email to *openshift@redhat.com*, on Twitter (@openshift), or in the *#openshift* channel on IRC's FreeNode network.

Conventions Used in This Book

The following typographical conventions are used in this book:

Italic
> Indicates new terms, URLs, email addresses, filenames, and file extensions.

`Constant width`
> Used for program listings, as well as within paragraphs to refer to program elements such as variable or function names, databases, data types, environment variables, statements, and keywords.

Constant width bold

> Shows commands or other text that should be typed literally by the user.

Constant width italic

> Shows text that should be replaced with user-supplied values or by values determined by context.

> This element signifies a tip or suggestion.

> This element indicates a warning or caution.

Using Code Examples

Supplemental material (code examples, exercises, etc.) is available for download at *https://github.com/oreillymedia/getting-started-with-openshift*.

This book is here to help you get your job done. In general, if example code is offered with this book, you may use it in your programs and documentation. You do not need to contact us for permission unless you're reproducing a significant portion of the code. For example, writing a program that uses several chunks of code from this book does not require permission. Selling or distributing a CD-ROM of examples from O'Reilly books does require permission. Answering a question by citing this book and quoting example code does not require permission. Incorporating a significant amount of example code from this book into your product's documentation does require permission.

We appreciate, but do not require, attribution. An attribution usually includes the title, author, publisher, and ISBN. For example: "*Getting Started with OpenShift* by Katie J. Miller and Steven Pousty (O'Reilly). Copyright 2014 Red Hat, Inc., 978-1-491-90047-5."

If you feel your use of code examples falls outside fair use or the permission given above, feel free to contact us at *permissions@oreilly.com*.

Safari® Books Online

 Safari Books Online is an on-demand digital library that delivers expert content in both book and video form from the world's leading authors in technology and business.

Technology professionals, software developers, web designers, and business and creative professionals use Safari Books Online as their primary resource for research, problem solving, learning, and certification training.

Safari Books Online offers a range of product mixes and pricing programs for organizations, government agencies, and individuals. Subscribers have access to thousands of books, training videos, and prepublication manuscripts in one fully searchable database from publishers like O'Reilly Media, Prentice Hall Professional, Addison-Wesley Professional, Microsoft Press, Sams, Que, Peachpit Press, Focal Press, Cisco Press, John Wiley & Sons, Syngress, Morgan Kaufmann, IBM Redbooks, Packt, Adobe Press, FT Press, Apress, Manning, New Riders, McGraw-Hill, Jones & Bartlett, Course Technology, and dozens more. For more information about Safari Books Online, please visit us online.

How to Contact Us

Please address comments and questions concerning this book to the publisher:

O'Reilly Media, Inc.
1005 Gravenstein Highway North
Sebastopol, CA 95472
800-998-9938 (in the United States or Canada)
707-829-0515 (international or local)
707-829-0104 (fax)

We have a web page for this book, where we list errata, examples, and any additional information. You can access this page at *http://oreil.ly/getting-started-with-openshift*.

To comment or ask technical questions about this book, send email to *bookquestions@oreilly.com*.

For more information about our books, courses, conferences, and news, see our website at *http://www.oreilly.com*.

Find us on Facebook: *http://facebook.com/oreilly*

Follow us on Twitter: *http://twitter.com/oreillymedia*

Watch us on YouTube: *http://www.youtube.com/oreillymedia*

Acknowledgments

A huge thank you must go the entire OpenShift team for allowing us to pester them with questions during the writing of this book. In particular, Grant Shipley, our supervisor, was instrumental in pushing us to write this and freeing up some of our time to get it done. A big thank you must also go to Michelle Brinich for working to get our book through all the hoops at Red Hat.

Furthermore, we would like to thank Brian Anderson from O'Reilly for keeping us on target with a short deadline and giving us great feedback.

Steven

I would like to thank Angelina, for her excellent humor, food, patience, and keeping me sane while I worked on the book. Thanks to my kids Fay, Tessa, and Felix for tolerating and understanding my sometimes grumpy moods (I hate writing) and not being able to watch *Cowboy Bebop* or *Korra* or go on a hike or shoot BB guns with you. I also want to thank all the developers who sat through my various workshops or talked to me on IRC—your feedback helped me refine my ideas for this book. Thanks to Katie for taking on writing this book with me and for being a partner in the creation and editing of the book. Finally, I would like to thank Hashem for giving me the capacity to write the book: B"H.

Katie

I would like to thank my husband, Brendan, for his love, support, and unwavering belief in me; I would not have had the capacity to undertake this or many of my other technical endeavors without you. I am also grateful to the rest of my family and circle of friends for their ongoing encouragement and support. Special mention goes to Gareth as parts of this book were written outside the ICU; my thoughts and prayers are with you for a speedy recovery. Finally, my thanks goes to Steve for all of his efforts—it was fun working together to pump out this book.

## CHAPTER 1

Introduction

Welcome to this "Impatient Beginner's Guide" to OpenShift. You have signed up for an account and now you are ready to create an application. Let's move right to covering the minimum background information you will need so you can get to building things.

What Is the Difference Between IaaS, PaaS, and SaaS?

Let's start by clearing up some "cloud computing" acronyms that people like to throw around.

Infrastructure as a Service (IaaS) is when a provider spins up computers for you on demand with certain predefined virtual hardware configurations. It is mainly targeted at system administrators and DevOps staff who used to *rack and stack* hardware. Probably the most famous of these services is Amazon EC2, but there is also Rackspace, Microsoft Azure, and Google Compute Engine, among others. The idea is that you specify the amount of RAM, CPU, and disk space you want in your "machine" and the provider spins it up for you in a matter of minutes.

This service is great since you no longer have to go through a long procurement process or fixed investment to obtain machines for your work. The drawback to this solution is that you are still responsible for installing and maintaining the operating system and server packages, configuring the network, and doing all the basic system administration. If you are reading this book, then system administration is probably not your area of expertise and you would likely rather spend your time writing code.

Software as a Service (SaaS) requires the least amount of maintenance and administration on your part. With SaaS you just sign up for the service and start using it. You may be able to make some customizations, but you're limited to what the service provider allows you to do. Common examples of SaaS are Gmail, Salesforce, and QuickBooks Online. While these services are useful because you can start working right away with little to configure or deploy, they are of limited use to programmers. They offer the least amount of customization of the three cloud services mentioned here. As Steve's kids' physical education teacher says: "You get what you get and you don't get upset."

Platform as a Service (PaaS) is the middle ground between IaaS and SaaS. It is primarily targeted at application developers and programmers. With PaaS, you issue a few commands (which could be in a web console) and the platform spins up the development environment along with all the "server" pieces you need to run your application. For example, in this book we are going to make a Python web application with a PostgreSQL database. To get all this spun up, you issue one command and OpenShift does all the networking and server installs, and creates a Git repository for you. The OpenShift administrators will keep the operating system up-to-date, manage the network, and do all the sys admin work—leaving the developer to focus on writing code.

The Three Versions of OpenShift

OpenShift is Red Hat's PaaS, and there are three different versions: OpenShift Origin, OpenShift Online, and OpenShift Enterprise (see Figure 1-1). OpenShift Origin, the free and open source version of OpenShift, is the upstream project for the other two versions. It is on GitHub (*http://openshift.github.io*) and released under an Apache 2 license. All changes to the code base go through the public repository, for both Red Hat and external developers. If you want to use this version you will have to install it on your own infrastructure. We are not going to cover the installation of the OpenShift PaaS in this book.

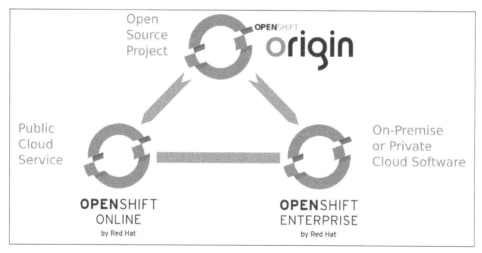

Figure 1-1. The relationship between the three versions of OpenShift

Approximately once every three weeks (the length of a sprint), Origin is packaged up and released as a new version of OpenShift Online. We are going to be using this version of OpenShift in the book. With Online, Red Hat takes care of hosting the PaaS on Amazon Web Services (AWS) and you just create an account for it. All the server work, such as updating the OS and managing networks, is covered by the OpenShift operations team. You are free to focus on your application and its code.

The final version is OpenShift Enterprise, which is currently released about once a quarter. This version of OpenShift allows you to take the PaaS and run it anywhere you want, from bare metal in your data center to Rackspace or AWS. It is a complete package with Red Hat Enterprise Linux and all the OpenShift bits on top of it. It is also fully supported by Red Hat and is intended for customers who want stability and a production-ready install out of the box. Since stability is paramount, some of the features found in Origin or Online may not be in Enterprise for a release or two. The great part about having Enterprise in-house is that it allows sys admins and DevOps staff to have control over "standard architecture" while still allowing developers to self-provision. Developers get all the speed and agility they want, without the usual wait for "machine" provisioning. It actually helps the sys admins and developers get along.

You can move applications between any of these versions of OpenShift, as long as the cartridges used are available on the versions between which you are migrating. This gives developers and companies a very nice hybrid cloud option. Developers and small teams can work on Online, perhaps using Online for some of the applications that allow for data in the public cloud. However, if they start developing an application that has more stringent data requirements, they can bring it back behind the company firewall, keeping the same development pattern they used for the Online platform. The Online version can also be used to try out a new technology, for example Node.js at a Java shop, with minimal risk and learning investment for the sys admins. Then, if the development team likes the new technology, they can demo the application to the decision makers and sys admins to show the value in bringing the technology in-house. The sys admins can use Red Hat's expertise in configuring the new technology on OpenShift to provide it internally. Since they have it in-house and it is standard Node.js, they can then tweak and tune it in a way that allows for rapid deployment to all internal projects using the new technology.

Choosing the Right Solution for You

As always with these questions, the optimal solution depends on the specifics of your use case. Maybe the decision has already been made for you—for example, if you work at a corporation that has already chosen OpenShift Enterprise and that is what you will be using. If you want the fewest management concerns, then you should look to Open-Shift Online. Everything will be managed by the OpenShift Operations team. The trade-off is that you have less control over how the system is set up, what cartridges are available, and how the network is configured.

If you want to be on the cutting edge of PaaS, you feel comfortable supporting yourself on Linux-based machines, and you want to provide your own "hardware," then running OpenShift Origin with Fedora or CentOS could be an option. On the other hand, if you want a more stable and supported version of OpenShift running Red Hat Enterprise Linux, then you are going to be interested in OpenShift Enterprise.

Given the state of developers, corporations, and the cloud, some good use cases for Online are hackathons, prototype projects, consulting houses, startups, smaller divisions in larger corporations, and students. OpenShift Origin might be good for a corporation trialing the notion of running its own PaaS, a hosting provider, or a university that wants to set up student experimentation. Please be aware that, given the trajectory of PaaS, there will probably be large corporations using public PaaS instances for production workloads within a year of the publication of this book. Steve is willing to bet a beer or a lemonade on it.

With that brief introduction, we are done talking about broad concepts and will now move into the discussion of concepts particular to OpenShift and how to get started.

Things to Understand

We know you are impatient and want to get started, but it is important for us to get some definitions cleared up first. It is also important to introduce some technology that you'll use throughout your development workflow. If you are comfortable with the technology feel free to skip right over that next section, but please make sure you understand the definitions.

Words You Need to Understand

There is some basic terminology that is specific to OpenShift or used specifically on the platform. It is important to clarify these terms since they will be used throughout the text:

Application
> This is your typical web application that will run on OpenShift. At this time, OpenShift is focused on hosting web applications. With this in mind, and to try to provide some security for your applications, the only ports exposed to incoming traffic are HTTP (80), HTTPS (443), and SSH (22). OpenShift also provides beta WebSocket (*http://en.wikipedia.org/wiki/WebSocket*) support on HTTP (8000) and HTTPS (8443).

Gear
> A gear is a server container with a set of resources that allows users to run their applications. Your gears run on OpenShift in the cloud. There are currently three gear types on OpenShift Online: small, medium, and large. Each size provides 1 GB

of disk space by default. The large gear has 2 GB of RAM, the medium gear has 1 GB of RAM, and the small gear has 512 MB of RAM.

Cartridge

To get a gear to do anything, you need to add a cartridge. Cartridges are the plug-ins that house the framework or components that can be used to create and run an application. One or more cartridges run on each gear, and the same cartridge can run on many gears for clustering or scaling. There are two kinds of cartridges:

Standalone

These are the languages or application servers that are set up to serve your web content, such as JBoss, Tomcat, Python, or Node.js. Having one of these cartridges is sufficient to run an application.

Embedded

An embedded cartridge provides functionality to enhance your application, such as a database or Cron, but cannot be used on its own to create an application.

Scalable application

Application scaling enables your application to react to changes in traffic and automatically allocate the necessary resources to handle your increased demand. The OpenShift infrastructure monitors incoming web traffic and automatically brings up new gears with the appropriate web cartridge online to handle more requests. When traffic decreases, the platform retires the extra resources. There is a web page dedicated to explaining how scaling works on OpenShift (*http://bit.ly/1gV8NYI*).

Client tools, Web Console, or Eclipse plug-ins

You can interact with the OpenShift platform via RHC client command-line tools you install on your local machine, the OpenShift Web Console, or a plug-in you install in Eclipse to interact with your application in the OpenShift cloud. The only time you must use these tools is when you are managing the infrastructure or components of your application. For example, you would use these tools when creating an application or embedding a new cartridge. The rest of your work with your application will happen through Git and SSH, which we describe in the following section.

Technology You Need to Understand

There is also some basic technology you need to be able to use to effectively work with OpenShift as a developer. The rest of this book will assume you understand this technology at a basic level.

SSH

SSH is a tool (*http://docstore.mik.ua/orelly/networking_2ndEd/ssh/ch01_01.htm*) you install on your local machine that allows you to log in to your OpenShift gears and have command-line access. With SSH, all interactions with the server are encrypted. Open-Shift also uses SSH keys to authenticate your login for both command-line access and Git interactions. With the use of keys, you never have to type in a password to connect to the server.

Once you SSH into your gear, you have all the access you need as an application developer; you can look at logs, change configuration for your app servers, and move files around. However, you are not an administrator on the gear; you cannot install new binaries using yum, you cannot change DNS settings, and you cannot get root access. One other benefit of SSH is that you can also use it to port forward, which "tricks" your local machine into thinking things running on your gear can be accessed locally. There is a whole section dealing with remote access over SSH (*https://www.openshift.com/developers/remote-access*) on OpenShift.com, and we discuss it further in Chapter 5. There is also an OpenShift blog post discussing SSH port forwarding (*https://www.open shift.com/blogs/getting-started-with-port-forwarding-on-openshift*). There are instructions on how to use port forwarding in Chapter 7.

Git

Git (*http://git-scm.com/*) is a program that provides distributed version control. You may have used Subversion, CVS, or Visual SourceSafe; these are centralized version control systems. With centralized systems there is a master server and everyone else has a copy of the code that they need to synchronize with the master. With Git, every repository, from the one on your laptop to the one on the server, is considered a legitimate master. Everything is kept in sync through patches sent between repositories. You can use Git like a pseudo-centralized version control system by having everyone on the team agree on "The Master." Wikipedia has a good discussion (*http://en.wikipedia.org/wiki/Distributed_revision_control*) about some of the differences between centralized and distributed version control systems.

The important thing to keep in mind with Git is that the Git repository on your machine is considered a repository, and you need to commit your changes there first. You have to add any new files and commit any changes on your local machine before you can push your changes to any other Git repository.

On OpenShift, when you spin up the primary application gear you create a Git repository on that gear that hosts all the code for your application. If you use the command-line tools or the Eclipse tools, at the end of application creation you clone the Git repository from the gear onto your local machine. We use SSH to secure all our Git transactions, so if you don't get your SSH keys set up properly you can't actually do any development work on your application. After the cloning, you now have two Git repositories:

- A remote repository on the OpenShift gear
- A local repository on your laptop or desktop

There are three basic commands you need to use to work with OpenShift:

`git add`
> Add a file to your local Git repository. Even if a file is in the directory representing your Git repo, it is *not* considered part of the repository until you add it.

`git commit`
> Commit any changes you have made to your local repository.

`git push`
> Push the changes from your local repository back up to the gear from which it was cloned.

If you are interested in learning more, there are several different (*http://bit.ly/1dubZuh*) decent documents (*http://bit.ly/1mjkIaS*) to get you going (*http://bit.ly/1r0Je1h*). If you are coming from Subversion land, there is even a Git introduction for you (*http://bit.ly/1gLk81Y*). The fine people at GitHub have also put together a nice collection of resources about Git (*http://bit.ly/O86g76*).

A quick note about the difference between Git and GitHub (*https://github.com/*). Git is the tool; GitHub is a site that allows for public and private hosting of Git repositories. GitHub also adds a lot of social features, making it very easy for developers to find and collaborate on code. We host many QuickStarts—Git repositories that are a shortcut to getting started with a framework or an application—on GitHub (*https://github.com/openshift/*). That said, there is no requirement to use GitHub with OpenShift, and your application repositories are private and only accessible to people with SSH access to your gear.

This chapter covered the minimal amount of background you need to get started creating applications. We didn't cover much information about how OpenShift is architected, its various pieces, or other tools you can use when working on the platform. Once you build a few applications, you can go on and read more about those topics *if* you need to. With all those preliminaries out of the way, let's move on to why you really got this book—time to create a web application!

## CHAPTER 2

Creating Applications

Since this is a guide for the impatient, we are going to dig right in and create our first application. In this chapter we are going to spin up a plain Python application without any code dependencies. Like we said in the Preface, we chose Python because it is easy to read. The goal is for you to get comfortable with the syntax for creating OpenShift applications; you do not need to know Python to understand this book. Again, we are just using Python to illustrate the patterns of working with OpenShift; this book will most definitely *not* make you a Python expert.

Preliminary Steps

Before you get started, you'll need to do two things:

- Sign up for an OpenShift account (*https://openshift.redhat.com/app/account/new*).
- Install the RHC command-line tools (*https://www.openshift.com/get-started#cli*). While you can also use the web interface or the Eclipse plug-in, we believe the command-line tools offer the best opportunity to experience the full power of developing applications on OpenShift. If you would like to know more about creating and managing your applications through the Web Console or an IDE, see the links in "Online Resources" on page x.

In the next section, we will explain the `rhc setup` command.

Setting Up the Command-Line Tools

Once you have installed the client tools, you need to configure them to work with your OpenShift Online account. To do this, use the following command:

```
$ rhc setup
```

Executing this command sets up your command-line tools to talk to the OpenShift servers. When you run this command, the following things will happen:

- RHC will talk to the OpenShift server and make sure your OpenShift username and password are valid. All the interactions between the command-line tools and the OpenShift servers use the OpenShift REST API (*http://red.ht/1fW9cQe*).

- RHC creates a token on your local machine that saves you from having to authenticate against the REST API each time. This token will expire after 30 days, forcing you to authenticate again.

- RHC will prompt you to create a namespace. Your namespace will be part of all your application URLs and has to be unique on OpenShift. Our recommendation is to make it short but somehow related to you. You can change it later, but it will change all your application URLs.

- Finally, the tool will check to see if you have an SSH key pair named *id_rsa* and *id_rsa.pub*. If you do, it will upload the public key (*.pub*) to the OpenShift server. If you don't have a key pair with these names it will create a pair for you and then ask to upload the public key. You need a key uploaded so you can carry out all the day-to-day development interactions with the server. After it uploads the key, your setup is complete.

Further Notes on SSH

If you ever find that SSH is failing or you are having trouble with key pairs, go ahead and run `rhc setup` again. SSH failing can also manifest in you not being able to `git push`, due to an authorization failure. The `setup` command actually carries out a bunch of different tests when it runs and it may be able to detect your problem. You can also use the `ssh` command in verbose mode (`ssh -v`) to see what keys it is trying to use.

If you are on Windows, you may be using *PuTTY* as your SSH client. Unfortunately for you, PuTTY uses a different kind of key-signing routine than OpenSSH, which is used by OpenShift. If you add your public PuTTY key to the Web Console you may be able to SSH into your application, but it is highly likely that your Git interactions will not work. You will need to convert your PuTTY public key into an OpenSSH-compatible key.

Make sure to protect your SSH private key. If somebody gains access to your private key, that person can then use it to log in to every site where you put the public key. Needless to say, that would be bad. On the other hand, don't worry about sharing your public key —it was intended to be put on plenty of other machines, some of which may be insecure.

You may be wondering why you need a password and an SSH key. The reason for this is that there are two different ways to interact with the server: *infrastructure* mode and *development* mode.

In infrastructure mode, you use the RHC command-line tools to create an application, allocate more gears, or add another cartridge. This is the only time you are required to use the command-line tools (or Web Console or IDE plug-in). The REST API used by the command-line tools uses the OpenShift username and password for authentication.

In development mode, you don't need to use the command-line tools; you can do all your work with SSH and Git. Both of these tools use your SSH key to let you interact directly with your gears. This includes interactions like using Git pushes, SSH tunneling, and connecting to your gear's console via SSH. When you SSH in, you can change some server configurations and look at your logs. This piece of OpenShift doesn't care about your username and password, and you will see the advantages of this later in the book. This is why you need an SSH key *and* a username and password.

Creating Your First Application

With our RHC setup complete, we are ready to create our first application. For the purposes of this book, we are going to create a Python application. In actuality you could use any of the supported web cartridges to make an application. The list of cartridges grows pretty rapidly, so if you want to see the full list of cartridges on OpenShift, please execute the following command:

```
$ rhc cartridge list
```

You can also create your own cartridges (*http://bit.ly/1l7Q1VN*). We are not going to cover how to create a cartridge in this book, since we consider that topic to be an advanced use case. Besides, if we talked about it here, how could you write about it when you write your OpenShift book? We cover much more about cartridges in "Finding Cartridges and QuickStarts" on page 32.

Before you make an application, use the command line to create or navigate into the directory where you would like your application code to be created. At the end of application creation, the command-line tools will clone the application's Git repository to your local machine in the same directory where you executed the command.

Let's create an app!

Here's the syntax for creating an OpenShift application:

```
$ rhc app create app_name web_language
```

or:

```
rhc app create app_name web_language other cartridges
```

And here is how we use this command to create an application named *insultapp* using the Python 2.7 cartridge:

```
[me@localhost ~]$ rhc app create insultapp python-2.7
```

```
Application Options
--------------------
Domain:     osbeginnerbook
Cartridges: python-2.7
Gear Size:  default
Scaling:    no

Creating application 'insultapp' ... done

Waiting for your DNS name to be available ... done

Cloning into 'insultapp'...
The authenticity of host 'insultapp-osbeginnerbook.rhcloud.com (19.66.2.6)'
can't be established.
RSA key fingerprint is 4e:65:76:72:47:6f:6e:6e:61:47:69:76:65:55:55:70.
Are you sure you want to continue connecting (yes/no)? yes
Warning: Permanently added 'insultapp-osbeginnerbook.rhcloud.com' (RSA) to the
list of known hosts.

Your application 'insultapp' is now available.

   URL:        http://insultapp-osbeginnerbook.rhcloud.com/
   SSH to:     6e7672676e61676976757570@insultapp-osbeginnerbook.rhcloud.com
   Git remote: ssh://6e7672676e61676976757570@insultapp-osbeginnerbook.
   rhcloud.com/~/git/insultapp.git/
   Cloned to:  /home/me/insultapp

Run 'rhc show-app insultapp' for more details about your app.
```

That's it! When the command finishes executing you will have an Apache HTTP server with *mod_wsgi* running in the cloud. It will have a public URL, which will have the form *http://insultapp-<namespace>.rhcloud.com*. It will also have a private Git repository that has been cloned to your local machine, in a directory with the same name as your application.

We could have made our app a scalable application (meaning each cartridge goes on its own gear) by passing in the -s flag. You would do this if you wanted to make sure your cartridges were not sharing resources or you wanted to enable the application server tier to scale (manually or automatically) from the database tier. We will discuss this further in the next section.

We could also pass in the -g flag to use gear sizes other than the default (small) size. On OpenShift Online's free tier you only have access to the small gears, but if you move into the paid tiers you can get a medium or large gear, which has more RAM. Please see "Reasons to Move to the Paid Tier" on page 15 to understand other reasons to move into the paid tier.

Finally, we could use the --from-code option to point to a publicly accessible Git repository to serve as the template for our application. We could have done that in this example, but we are going to build the example application by hand instead. One caveat with this flag is that when OpenShift tries to create the gear, the application has to download and build the Git repository within a particular time period. If the `rhc cre ate` command times out before the build and deploy occurs, then OpenShift will roll back the entire application and you will be left with nothing except the bitter taste of disappointment. Use this feature with caution for now.

 To delete OpenShift applications, use the command `rhc app de lete`. This will trash all your resources in the application on the OpenShift servers and allow you to use the resources in a new application.

Go ahead and look at your web page. What you should see is the template page created for all OpenShift applications (Figure 2-1). This page is pretty generic. In the next chapter, we will modify the application and deploy the code changes. Take a step back and marvel at what you just did. With one command you spun up Apache with *mod_wsgi*, allocated disk space, configured logging, configured Linux permissions, registered an IP address with a DNS server, and made both a remote and a local Git repository. With that little bit of typing you have a fully functional application development hosting environment. This is the magic of OpenShift, and your development process may never be the same again.

Figure 2-1. What your first application looks like

Autoscaling and Why You Should Use It by Default

OpenShift is the only PaaS on the market that provides autoscaling at the application tier. We have not used it here for the sake of simplicity, but if we were going to run an app in the "real world," we would make it scalable. When you make an application scalable, a software-based load balancer called *HAProxy* will be added to the same gear as the application server. All web traffic to the application will then be routed through HAProxy. Currently, if the number of active connections goes above 16—whether they are regular HTTP or WebSocket connections—HAProxy will trigger the creation of another application gear. OpenShift will spin up another app server gear, rsync the code over to the new gear, plug the gear into HAProxy, and then start using it to serve connections. If the connections later drop back below the threshold for long enough for it not to be considered random noise, HAProxy will trigger the draining of connections and OpenShift will spin down the gear.

All of this happens without any human intervention, so you do not have to wake up in the middle of the night or take time out from sailing around the world on your yacht (wouldn't that be nice). Of course, OpenShift lets you set a maximum number of gears for application server use so you are not surprised by some large bill at the end of the month, thereby ending your yacht trip.

As we have taught more and more classes and seen more and more people using Open-Shift, we have arrived at the conclusion that almost all apps should be created as scalable applications. There are several reasons for this:

- Your application server, your database server, and any other servers you put in your application will each go on their own gears and therefore not compete for disk, memory, or other resources. This will give you much better performance compared to nonscaling, where they all run in the same gear.

- It gives you more flexibility if you start to experience more load on your application. You can set the scaling limits for the application tier to accommodate the new traffic.

- It will allow you to scale up manually if you know a big event is coming up and you want to warm up the servers beforehand.

- There is no command to make a nonscalable application into a scalable application. If you want to make a nonscalable app scalable, you will need to snapshot it, spin up a new scalable application, and then restore it to the new application (see "Application Snapshots with RHC" on page 71 for information about snapshots).

You are given enough resources in the free tier to make your application scalable, so there is really no reason why you shouldn't do this by default.

Reasons to Move to the Paid Tier

Everything we do in this book can be carried out using the free tier of OpenShift, but there are strong reasons why you might want to move into one of the paid tiers as your application becomes more serious. We will call out some of the benefits as we discuss topics in the following chapters, such as the ability to use your own SSL certificates. However, for the sake of gathering them in one place, we have included a short list here:

1. Your application will never be idled. Currently on the free tier, if there are no HTTP connections to your application for 48 hours, OpenShift idles the gear. Idling means OpenShift will serialize the entire application to disk. The next HTTP request to the application will have to wait while OpenShift deserializes the application. Please be aware that the time before idling could change; look at the OpenShift website for the latest information. If you are a paid-tier user, then your users will never experience the delay of the application coming back from idling.

2. You gain the ability to buy more gears, thereby allowing you to create more applications. With more gears you can also allow your applications to scale to handle more traffic.

3. You gain the ability to buy larger gears, which can be crucial for memory-hungry application servers.

4. You gain the ability to purchase premium application servers for more than three gears or on larger gears, such as JBoss EAP or Zend Server. You get to use these application servers on three small gears in the free tier, but the paid tier allows you to buy more and put them on more appropriately sized gears.

5. You gain the ability to get access to more disk space, beyond the 1 GB that comes with the free tier.

6. You can use your own SSL certificates with your custom domain names.

7. Some of the tiers provide the ability to open support tickets.

There is certainly no requirement to use the paid tier, but there are numerous reasons you may find yourself wanting to take advantage of what it has to offer.

## CHAPTER 3

Making Code Modifications

In Chapter 2 we used OpenShift and a single RHC command to create a Python application running in the cloud. In a matter of seconds the application was live on the Internet; when we visited its URL we got back the OpenShift equivalent of a *Hello World* page, including some useful information on what to do next. Spinning up an application quickly and easily like this is pretty cool, but a static page can only entertain for so long. In this chapter we will modify the default application to do something more exciting and deploy the changes to OpenShift.

Cloning Code to Your Local Machine

When you create an OpenShift application with the RHC command-line tools, by default the new Git repository created on the OpenShift gear will be cloned to your local machine. The contents will end up in a new directory with the same name as the application, created inside the directory in which you ran the `rhc app create` command. If you would like the repository to be cloned to a different location, specify this by adding the `--repo` *repo_dir_path* option to your `rhc app create` command; the repository contents will be cloned into the directory specified, which should either be empty or not yet exist. If you do not wish to clone the Git repository as part of the app creation process, you can add the `--no-git` flag.

If you choose not to clone the OpenShift application repository when you create the app, or something goes wrong and the clone fails, you can clone it later using the command `rhc git-clone`. This is a wrapper for the standard `git clone` command that provides some extra benefits: you can specify what to clone by using the application's name, rather than its full Git URL, and it adds some RHC configuration data to the Git repository config. This means that you can run RHC commands from within the cloned directory without having to specify the application to which you wish them to apply with `-a` *appname*. Where RHC commands shown in this book omit the `-a` *appname* option, it is because they are being run within an app repository cloned via RHC, either with `rhc app create` or `rhc git-clone`.

To view the Git URL for your OpenShift application, run the command `rhc app show -a` *appname*.

 In order to clone an application repository, you must have supplied OpenShift with an SSH public key for the machine on which you are working. If you have not yet done this, run the command `rhc setup`. See Chapter 2 for more information.

Modifying Application Code

Once you have a local copy of the OpenShift application repository you can modify the code using whatever tool you prefer: a command-line text editor, a graphical editor, or an IDE. For our example application, we will start by making a few changes to add and utilize the Python Flask microframework. Writing raw Web Server Gateway Interface (WSGI) apps is not much fun. Flask is a lightweight alternative that will give us just enough support to fulfill our app's main aim: insulting people. To learn more about Flask, see its website (*http://flask.pocoo.org*).

First up, we need to add Flask as a dependency. To do this, we navigate to the local cloned *insultapp* repository and open the *setup.py* file with our chosen editor (long live the Vim, though some of us believe Nano rules). In this file we can set the application name and other details; the most significant change to make, though, is uncommenting the `install_requires` line and replacing Django with Flask 0.10.1. Our resulting `setup` section looks like this:

```
setup(name='Insult App',
      version='1.0',
      description='Insults you',
      author='Katie and Steve',
      author_email='example@example.com',
      url='http://www.python.org/sigs/distutils-sig/',
      install_requires=['Flask==0.10.1'],
      )
```

The next file we need to edit is *wsgi/application*. It contains the HTML for the "Welcome to your Python application on OpenShift" page we saw in Chapter 2. We do not need any of the template code, so we delete everything beneath the comment lines marked as *IMPORTANT*. Beneath the comment, we add the line `from routes import app as application`, referencing the application code we are about to add next. Here is the source of the resulting *application* file:

```
#!/usr/bin/python
import os
```

```
virtenv = os.environ['OPENSHIFT_PYTHON_DIR'] + '/virtenv/'
virtualenv = os.path.join(virtenv, 'bin/activate_this.py')
try:
    execfile(virtualenv, dict(__file__=virtualenv))
except IOError:
    pass
#
# IMPORTANT: Put any additional includes below this line.  If placed above this
# line, it's possible required libraries won't be in your searchable path.
#
from routes import app as application
```

Finally, we add a new file in the *wsgi* directory called *routes.py*. This contains a single route for the application's root directory, which maps to an `insult` function that returns the mildly irritating string, "Hello, code monkey!" Here is the code:

```
import os
from flask import Flask

app = Flask(__name__)
# Keeps Flask from swallowing error messages
app.config['PROPAGATE_EXCEPTIONS'] = True

@app.route("/")
def insult():
    return "Hello, code monkey!"

if __name__ == "__main__":
    app.run()
```

In *routes.py* we create a Flask application type called `app`. From there we use annotations to define that HTTP requests to the root URL get handled by the function `insult`. The *application* file loads the Python virtual environment (a mechanism for having different Python libraries on the same machine) and imports the `app` from the `routes` module defined in *routes.py*.

Now that we have made some changes to the application code base, we should commit them to the local Git repository. We can do that with the following Git commands: `add` to add the changes to the repository index, and `commit` to record the new contents of the index. It is good practice to use the `git status` command before each one to make sure you are clear on what is happening, although for brevity this is not shown here:

```
[me@localhost ~/insultapp]$ git add -A
[me@localhost ~/insultapp]$ git commit -m "Added Flask microframework"
[master b1d87e3] Added Flask microframework
 3 files changed, 32 insertions(+), 315 deletions(-)
 rewrite wsgi/application (99%)
 create mode 100644 wsgi/routes.py
```

The code changes are now committed on our local machine, but our OpenShift app remains unaffected. In the next section, we will push our modifications to the cloud.

Building and Deploying Your Code

Once you have committed your code changes, you can deploy them to OpenShift with just one command: `git push`. There is no special binary or secret sauce involved; it is just pure Git and SSH. If we run the command `git status`, we can see that we have modifications ready and raring to go. The `git push` command sends them on their merry way up into the cloud:

```
[me@localhost ~/insultapp]$ git status
# On branch master
# Your branch is ahead of 'origin/master' by 1 commit.
#   (use "git push" to publish your local commits)
#
nothing to commit, working directory clean
[me@localhost ~/insultapp]$ git push
```

We have not included the full output of the `push` command here as it was quite lengthy, but here are some choice snippets:

```
remote: Stopping PYTHON cart
...
remote: Building git ref 'master', commit b1d87e3
...
remote: Installed /var/lib/openshift/6e7672676e61676976757570/app-root/runtime
/repo
remote: Processing dependencies for Insult-App==1.0
...
remote: Processing Flask-0.10.1.tar.gz
...
remote: Preparing build for deployment
...
remote: Activating deployment
...
remote: Starting PYTHON cart
remote: Result: success
remote: Activation status: success
remote: Deployment completed with status: success
```

Note that each time new code is deployed, the directory on the gear containing the current copy of the Git repository is blown away and then replaced with an updated copy, so anything stored there between deployments will be lost. We explain where you can store files persistently in Chapter 8.

By default, pushing code changes to the OpenShift repository will also trigger a deployment; however, this behavior can be changed. See Chapter 9 to learn how.

As we can see from the console output, when code is pushed to OpenShift it kicks off a build lifecycle, which has build and deployment phases. This lifecycle will differ slightly depending on the application cartridge in use, whether or not the app is scalable, and whether or not a builder cartridge such as Jenkins is included. In the case of our example app, the Python cartridge is stopped, the Git repository is cloned, a series of Python-specific processes occur to fetch dependencies and prepare the app, the resulting build is deployed, and the cartridge is restarted. You will learn more about most of these other pieces of application deployment in later chapters. In the next section we will talk about how you can write scripts to hook into various phases of the build.

Once this cycle is complete, we can visit our application URL in a browser and are now greeted with "Hello, code monkey!" (see Figure 3-1).

Figure 3-1. The Flask application in action

Action Hook Scripts

OpenShift cartridges are designed to take care of the major tasks required to build and deploy a web application. If there are actions you want to perform as part of the build lifecycle that go beyond the basics, you can include these in action hook scripts.

Action hook scripts are included as part of your application Git repository, in the *.openshift/action_hooks* directory. Different cartridges may support different hooks, depending on their build lifecycles; however, they should all include pre_build, build, deploy, and post_deploy, as well as pre and post hooks for the start, stop, restart, reload, and tidy actions.

To run code at a particular time in the lifecycle, place a script in the *action_hooks* directory with the same name as the phase when you want it to be executed. The script can be written in Shell, Python, PHP, Ruby, or any other scripting language installed in the OpenShift environment that you can reference. It does not matter what language you chose for your web application; all of these scripting environments are still available to run on your gear. The script should be executable; run the `chmod x` *scriptname* command to ensure this.

 Windows users may find that permissions they set on their action hook scripts are lost when the scripts are pushed to OpenShift with Git. To fix this issue, run the command `git update-index --chmod= +x .openshift/action_hooks/*` and push the scripts again.

Action hook scripts need to be added and committed in Git just like any other repository file. When they are pushed to the cloud, you will see any effects as the build lifecycle runs. For example, if you delete files in the */tmp* directory as part of an action hook, the `git push` output will echo the result of that command unless you tell your script to swallow output.

Hot-Deploying Code

When we pushed our code changes to the example application, we saw that the Python cartridge was stopped while the app was built and deployed, and then started back up again. If there had been a database cartridge installed in our application, it would have been stopped as well. This meant our application was unavailable for that time; if we had hit the URL at that moment, we would have received a 503 Service Unavailable message. In addition, for many of OpenShift's programming languages, you do not need to stop the server to deploy new code on the server. Going through a start/stop cycle for the application server significantly slows down the deployment experience.

We want to properly insult people rather than scaring them away with server error status codes, so our next code change will be to add a marker file to tell the platform to hot deploy the code. This signals that OpenShift should deploy new application versions without restarting the server. The hot deployment option is available on most of the core OpenShift application cartridges; the JBoss, Tomcat, PHP, Zend, Perl, Ruby, and Python cartridges all support this. (See "Using Marker Files" on page 45 for more information about marker files.) Enabling hot deployment is as simple as creating an empty file named *hot_deploy* in the *.openshift/markers* directory, adding it to the local repository with `git add`, doing a `git commit`, and then finally executing a `git push`:

```
[me@localhost ~/insultapp]$ touch .openshift/markers/hot_deploy
[me@localhost ~/insultapp]$ git add .openshift/markers/hot_deploy
[me@localhost ~/insultapp]$ git commit -m "Changing application to hot deploy"
```

There are times when you want the server to be stopped and then started again, such as when making changes to *server.xml* in a Java application: you need the application server to restart in order to pick up the changes. There might also be times when you believe a bug in the code you are deploying or running has crashed the application server. Please remember to remove or rename the *hot_deploy* file, git add, git commit, and *then* git push in this situation. This is a sometimes-forgotten problem that has bitten at least one of your gentle authors more than once.

Our app is looking pretty good now, but a single canned insult will get old fast. We will make things more entertaining by adding some randomization, Elizabethan style. There is a list of insulting Shakespearean words that has been floating around the Internet practically since it was a twinkle in someone's eye (no, not Al Gore). There are two columns of adjectives and one column of nouns; the idea is to combine one word from each column. Our next step is to gather a few insulting words and add a *wsgi/insulter.py* file to encapsulate the serious business logic of contempt:

```python
from random import choice

def insult():
    return "Thou " + generate_insult() + "!"

def named_insult(name):
    return name + ", thou " + generate_insult() + "!"

def generate_insult():
    first_adjs = ["artless", "bawdy", "beslubbering", "bootless", "churlish"]
    second_adjs = ["base-court", "bat-fowling", "beef-witted", "beetle-headed",
     "boil-brained"]
    nouns = ["apple-john", "baggage", "barnacle", "bladder", "boar-pig"]

    return choice(first_adjs) + " " + choice(second_adjs) + " " + choice(nouns)
```

We use the choice function in the random module to select a random element in the Python lists, such as first_adjs. Next, we change the code in *wsgi/routes.py* to make use of our new functions:

```python
import os
from flask import Flask
import insulter

app = Flask(__name__)
# Keeps Flask from swallowing error messages
app.config['PROPAGATE_EXCEPTIONS'] = True

@app.route("/")
def insult():
    return insulter.insult()
```

```
@app.route("/<name>")
def insult_name(name):
    return insulter.named_insult(name)

if __name__ == "__main__":
    app.run()
```

Notice we import the `insulter` module (the file named *insulter.py*) and then use the two insult-constructing functions to generate our insults. You can also see that in the second `@app.route` we are grabbing any text after the / and making it available to the function `insult_name` as a parameter called `name`. We added this function for cases when only a personalized insult will do.

We add and commit those changes to the Git repository, and then the final step is to `git push` our latest two commits. The output from OpenShift shows that the server has not been stopped and restarted because hot deployment is enabled:

```
remote: Not stopping cartridge python because hot deploy is enabled
...
remote: Not starting cartridge python because hot deploy is enabled
```

Once the new code has hit the cloud, we can refresh the app for some random Shakespearean insult fun (see Figure 3-2).

Figure 3-2. A random insult from the hot-deployed app

In this chapter we showed how to modify OpenShift application starter code, spicing up our Python demo app with logic to insult its users. We achieved this with Git commands including `add`, `status`, `commit`, `push`, and, with the help of RHC, `clone`. We also explained how we can add custom scripts to the application lifecycle with action hooks, and how to use a marker file to configure an app to hot deploy.

## CHAPTER 4

Adding Application Components

OpenShift cartridges provide the components for building your application infrastructure. Our example Python app currently utilizes a single cartridge, Python 2.7. In this chapter, we will demonstrate how to add cartridges that provide additional capabilities, such as data storage, task scheduling, and monitoring. We will also explain how to find and use third-party cartridges created by the open-source community or OpenShift partner organizations.

 This chapter shows how to add cartridges to an OpenShift application after it has been created. However, you can also select multiple cartridges when you create your app. To do this, add the extra cartridge names or URLs after the primary cartridge name. For example, to create a PHP 5.4 application with Cron and a MySQL 5.5 database, you could use the following command:

```
rhc app create appname php-5.4 mysql-5.5 cron-1.4
```

Database-Related Cartridges

The cartridges most commonly added to OpenShift applications after creation are database cartridges, such as PostgreSQL, MySQL, and MongoDB. If the application is not scalable, the database cartridge will be installed on the same gear as the primary application cartridge. If the application is scalable, the database cartridge will be added on its own gear. This enables the gear hosting the application cartridge to be replicated, without affecting the database. It also prevents the application server and the database from sharing the memory and disk space of a single gear.

Cartridges can be added with the command rhc cartridge add, and removed with rhc cartridge remove. Other RHC cartridge management commands include list, status, start, restart, stop, and storage; `rhc cartridge --help` will display the full list of options.

Here we add a PostgreSQL 9.2 cartridge to our running example, Insult App:

```
[me@localhost ~/insultapp]$ rhc cartridge add postgresql-9.2

Adding postgresql-9.2 to application 'insultapp' ... done

postgresql-9.2 (PostgreSQL 9.2)
-------------------------------
  Gears:          Located with python-2.7
  Connection URL: postgresql://$OPENSHIFT_POSTGRESQL_DB_HOST:
  $OPENSHIFT_POSTGRESQL_DB_PORT
  Database Name:  insultapp
  Password:       SLat4aTfsSt1
  Username:       adminm4rvN42

PostgreSQL 9.2 database added.  Please make note of these credentials:

  Root User: adminm4rvN42
  Root Password: SLat4aTfsSt1
  Database Name: insultapp

Connection URL: postgresql://$OPENSHIFT_POSTGRESQL_DB_HOST:
$OPENSHIFT_POSTGRESQL_DB_PORT
```

We can see from the output that the PostgreSQL cartridge has been added and is located on the same gear as the Python cartridge; this is because our demo application is not scalable. RHC has also displayed some useful information about the database set-up, including the database root user's username and password.

There are multiple ways to connect to your OpenShift database. Spoiler alert: we will show you how to connect to a DB in your application code in Chapter 6; there are some other topics we need to cover first before we get there. We will demonstrate how to connect to the gear hosting the database via SSH and how to view the environment variables related to database (and other) cartridges in Chapter 5. To find out how to use port forwarding to connect to an OpenShift database, see Chapter 7.

There are additional cartridges you can add to your OpenShift application to help you manage some databases: for example, the phpMyAdmin, RockMongo, and MongoDB Monitoring Service cartridges. See "Finding Cartridges and QuickStarts" on page 32 for tips on where to find OpenShift cartridges.

Nondatabase Cartridges

Our discussion so far has been focused on OpenShift cartridges that provide programming language runtimes, application servers, web frameworks, and databases. These are the major building blocks of OpenShift applications, but the platform can also provide complementary functionality. At the end of the previous section, we briefly mentioned some of the cartridges available to assist with database administration and management. In this section, we will examine some of the other cartridges you may like to add to your app to facilitate tasks such as job scheduling, continuous integration, and metrics collection.

Cron

The Cron cartridge allows users to schedule jobs to be executed periodically, using the Linux `cron` utility. This tool can be used for tasks such as deleting temporary files, generating reports, backing up data, or Rickrolling (*http://en.wikipedia.org/wiki/Rick rolling*) friends regularly. To use `cron`, first add the Cron cartridge to your application with the `rhc cartridge add` command, as shown here for our Insult App:

```
[me@localhost ~/insultapp]$ rhc cartridge add cron
Using cron-1.4 (Cron 1.4) for 'cron'
Adding cron-1.4 to application 'insultapp' ... done

cron-1.4 (Cron 1.4)
-------------------
  Gears: Located with python-2.7, postgresql-9.2

To schedule your scripts to run on a periodic basis, add the scripts to
your application's .openshift/cron/{minutely,hourly,daily,weekly,monthly}/
directories (and commit and redeploy your application).

Example: A script .openshift/cron/hourly/crony added to your application
         will be executed once every hour.
         Similarly, a script .openshift/cron/weekly/chronograph added
         to your application will be executed once every week.
```

If we run the `rhc app show` command, we can see that our example application still has one gear but now lists three cartridges, Python 2.7, PostgreSQL 9.2, and Cron 1.4:

```
[me@localhost ~/insultapp]$ rhc app show
insultapp @ http://insultapp-osbeginnerbook.rhcloud.com/
(uuid: 6e7672676e61676976757570)
---------------------------------------------------------------------
  Domain:   osbeginnerbook
  Created:  Mar 14  1:59 PM
  Gears:    1 (defaults to small)
  Git URL:  ssh://6e7672676e61676976757570@insultapp-osbeginnerbook.rhcloud
  .com/~/git/insultapp.git/
  SSH:      6e7672676e61676976757570@insultapp-osbeginnerbook.rhcloud.com
```

```
Deployment: auto (on git push)

python-2.7 (Python 2.7)
-----------------------
  Gears: Located with postgresql-9.2, cron-1.4

postgresql-9.2 (PostgreSQL 9.2)
-------------------------------
  Gears:            Located with python-2.7, cron-1.4
  Connection URL: postgresql://$OPENSHIFT_POSTGRESQL_DB_HOST:
  $OPENSHIFT_POSTGRESQL_DB_PORT
  Database Name:  insultapp
  Password:       SLat4aTfsSt1
  Username:       adminm4rvN42

cron-1.4 (Cron 1.4)
-------------------
  Gears: Located with python-2.7, postgresql-9.2
```

To make use of our new Cron cartridge, we need to place a script in our local Git repository in one of the *.openshift/cron* directories. The directory we choose will dictate whether the job is performed every minute, hour, day, week, or month. The script needs to be executable (chmod +x *scriptname*) and should be added, committed, and pushed with Git, as described in Chapter 3.

Here is an example script that we will set to run every minute, so that it sends some special output to the cartridge log directory every half an hour:

```
#!/bin/bash
# .openshift/cron/minutely/ricktock

MIN=$(date '+%M')
LOG=${OPENSHIFT_PYTHON_LOG_DIR}/ricktock.log
MSG1="Never gonna give you up\nNever gonna let you down\nNever gonna run around
and desert you"
MSG2="Never gonna make you cry\nNever gonna say goodbye\nNever gonna tell a lie
and hurt you"

if [ $MIN == 15 ]; then
  echo -e `date` $MSG1 >> $LOG
fi

if [ $MIN == 45 ]; then
  echo -e `date` $MSG2 >> $LOG
fi

exit
```

Now we add this script, called *ricktock*, to our example application on OpenShift:

```
[me@localhost ~/insultapp]$ chmod +x .openshift/cron/minutely/ricktock
[me@localhost ~/insultapp]$ git add .openshift/cron/minutely/ricktock
```

```
[me@localhost ~/insultapp]$ git commit -m "Adding ricktock minutely Cron script"
[master 2548477] Adding ricktock minutely Cron script
 1 file changed, 18 insertions(+)
 create mode 100755 .openshift/cron/minutely/ricktock
[me@localhost ~/insultapp]$ git push
```

Once the script has been deployed (and we've waited a little while), we can see the glorious result in the application log output with the `rhc tail` command. This command reads the last lines of all the files in the log directory and sends the output to your local console:

```
[me@localhost ~/insultapp]$ rhc tail
==> python/logs/ricktock.log <==
Fri Mar 14 14:15:44 EST 2014 Never gonna give you up
Never gonna let you down
Never gonna run around and desert you
```

For more information about viewing application logs, see "Log Access" on page 43. For an example of a Cron script to back up your OpenShift database, see "Writing a Cron Script" on page 73.

Continuous Integration

Another capability you may wish to add to your OpenShift applications is support for continuous integration. In this section we will show how to create an instance of the open source Jenkins (*http://jenkins-ci.org/*) continuous integration server on OpenShift, as well as how to configure your apps to build on this server. It is also possible to build OpenShift applications on Travis CI (*http://www.openshift.com/quickstarts/travis-ci-on-openshift*), but that is an advanced discussion so it will not be covered in this book.

Before we can configure our OpenShift application to build on Jenkins, we need to create a Jenkins server app. While we are using a small gear again, given how memory-intensive Jenkins can be we highly recommend using a medium or large gear if you want to make heavy use of it. The process for this is the same as for any other OpenShift application; we can use `rhc app create`, as shown here:

```
[me@localhost ~/insultapp]$ cd ..
[me@localhost ~]$ rhc app create jenkins jenkins-1
Application Options
-------------------
  Domain:     osbeginnerbook
  Cartridges: jenkins-1
  Gear Size:  default
  Scaling:    no

Creating application 'jenkins' ... done

  Jenkins created successfully.  Please make note of these credentials:

  User: admin
```

```
    Password: iYddhaBUvg2m

Note:  You can change your password at: https://jenkins-osbeginnerbook.rhcloud
.com/me/configure

Waiting for your DNS name to be available ... done

Cloning into 'jenkins'...
The authenticity of host 'jenkins-osbeginnerbook.rhcloud.com (19.77.5.25)' can't
be established.
RSA key fingerprint is 54:68:65:46:6f:72:63:65:69:73:73:74:72:6f:6e:67.
Are you sure you want to continue connecting (yes/no)? yes
Warning: Permanently added 'jenkins-osbeginnerbook.rhcloud.com,19.77.5.25' (RSA)
to the list of known hosts.

Your application 'jenkins' is now available.

    URL:        http://jenkins-osbeginnerbook.rhcloud.com/
    SSH to:     4e6f72726973206265617264@jenkins-osbeginnerbook.rhcloud.com
    Git remote: ssh://4e6f72726973206265617264@jenkins-osbeginnerbook.rhcloud.com/
    ~/git/jenkins.git/
    Cloned to:  /home/codemiller/code/book/jenkins

Run 'rhc show-app jenkins' for more details about your app.
```

Once we have a Jenkins server in our OpenShift domain we can add the client Jenkins cartridge to our example application. The client cartridge is used to indicate that you want to use your domain's Jenkins server to build this application:

```
[me@localhost ~]$ cd insultapp
[me@localhost ~/insultapp]$ rhc cartridge add jenkins-client-1
Adding jenkins-client-1 to application 'insultapp' ... done

jenkins-client-1 (Jenkins Client)
---------------------------------
    Gears:   Located with python-2.7, postgresql-9.2, cron-1.4
    Job URL: https://jenkins-osbeginnerbook.rhcloud.com/job/insultapp-build/

Associated with job 'insultapp-build' in Jenkins server.
```

Adding the client cartridge has prompted OpenShift to create a job for the *insult* application, called *insultapp-build*, on the Jenkins server. When we push changes to OpenShift, the application will now be built on Jenkins. If the build and any tests are successful, the result will be deployed to the application gear or gears. If the build is unsuccessful, the OpenShift application will continue to run without downtime.

 For more information about Jenkins, see the "Build with Jenkins" (*https://www.openshift.com/jenkins*) section on OpenShift.com.

Metrics and Monitoring

Another category of cartridges you may wish to add to support your application is cartridges for metrics collection and monitoring.

At the time of writing, the OpenShift Metrics cartridge was at version 0.1 and still under development. It is designed to be able to be embedded with any primary application cartridge type. To add it to your application, use the command rhc cartridge add metrics-0.1 -a *appname*. Once it is installed, you can access real-time statistics about your application's resource usage at *http://**appname-domain**.rhcloud.com/metrics*, as shown in Figure 4-1. The cartridge gives visibility to some key information, including the amount of CPU and RAM use (and how that relates to the gear limit), how much swap space is being utilized, application process IDs, and whether or not your application is in an idle state.

Figure 4-1. The OpenShift Metrics cartridge interface

Another monitoring option is the Monit cartridge (*http://bit.ly/1fEeEpO*), which uses the open source Monit process supervision tool (*http://mmonit.com/monit/*). The cartridge comes with some predefined rules for checking OpenShift application availability, storage, and memory use. It will send email notifications when significant events occur, such as your gear reaching 80 percent of its quota or your app becoming unavailable. Additional rules can be added to check different application metrics and to take actions based on the results, such as restarting a cartridge. See "Adding Third-Party Cartridges" on page 35 to learn how to install Monit and other community cartridges.

If your OpenShift application is scalable, it will include the HAProxy cartridge for load balancing. Although its primary function is not monitoring, it is worth noting that HAProxy includes a page that allows you to view some useful data about your application, available at *http://**appname-domain**.rhcloud.com/haproxy-status*. This status page shows how many application gears you have running, if all the gears are online, how many users are connecting to your app, and how much data the app is streaming.

> For those using MongoDB, another monitoring cartridge that may come in handy is the MongoDB Monitoring Service (MMS) cartridge (*http://bit.ly/1cEYzjV*).

Given that OpenShift is open source, new cartridges are being developed by the community all the time; the next section offers tips on finding them and shows how to utilize third-party cartridges.

> OpenShift partner organization New Relic offers a mature application monitoring solution, with free standard accounts available. There was no New Relic OpenShift cartridge at the time of writing, but there are instructions on how to add New Relic to your Java/JBoss application (*http://bit.ly/1iJheJI*). Another OpenShift partner, AppDynamics, has created an OpenShift QuickStart (*http://bit.ly/1kQPpUe*) for its monitoring software.

Finding Cartridges and QuickStarts

One of the joyous consequences of having an open source platform is that the community is always creating exciting new things for it. When you run the command `rhc cartridge list`, the result shows supported cartridges (Table 4-1 shows the list as of March 2014); these are the components that are maintained by Red Hat and receive updates such as security patches. However, this is not the extent of the cartridges available. There are many more OpenShift cartridges that have been created by the community and partner organizations. There are also many QuickStarts (*https://www.open shift.com/quickstarts*), which combine one or more cartridges with preconfigured code and libraries to enable you to quickly and easily launch a given application on OpenShift.

Table 4-1. Supported cartridges for OpenShift Online (as of March 2014)

```
[me@localhost ~]$ rhc cartridge list
```

jbossas-7	JBoss Application Server 7	web
jbosseap-6 (*)	JBoss Enterprise Application Platform 6	web
jenkins-1	Jenkins Server	web
nodejs-0.10	Node.js 0.10	web
nodejs-0.6	Node.js 0.6	web
perl-5.10	Perl 5.10	web
php-5.3	PHP 5.3	web
zend-5.6	PHP 5.3 with Zend Server 5.6	web
php-5.4	PHP 5.4	web
zend-6.1	PHP 5.4 with Zend Server 6.1	web
python-2.6	Python 2.6	web
python-2.7	Python 2.7	web
python-3.3	Python 3.3	web
ruby-1.8	Ruby 1.8	web
ruby-1.9	Ruby 1.9	web
jbossews-1.0	Tomcat 6 (JBoss EWS 1.0)	web
jbossews-2.0	Tomcat 7 (JBoss EWS 2.0)	web
diy-0.1	Do-It-Yourself 0.1	web
10gen-mms-agent-0.1	10gen Mongo Monitoring Service Agent	addon
cron-1.4	Cron 1.4	addon
jenkins-client-1	Jenkins Client	addon
mongodb-2.4	MongoDB 2.4	addon
mysql-5.1	MySQL 5.1	addon
mysql-5.5	MySQL 5.5	addon
metrics-0.1	OpenShift Metrics 0.1	addon
phpmyadmin-4	phpMyAdmin 4.0	addon
postgresql-8.4	PostgreSQL 8.4	addon
postgresql-9.2	PostgreSQL 9.2	addon
rockmongo-1.1	RockMongo 1.1	addon
switchyard-0	SwitchYard 0.8.0	addon
haproxy-1.4	Web Load Balancer	addon

(*) denotes a cartridge with additional usage costs.

Web cartridges can be added only to new applications.

There are several places you can go to look for OpenShift cartridges and QuickStarts. A decent place to start is OpenShift.com; some downloadable cartridges (*https://www.openshift.com/developers/download-cartridges*) and many QuickStarts (*https://www.openshift.com/quickstarts*) are listed there. You can browse the OpenShift-maintained offerings and some partner and community offerings in the OpenShift Web Console (*https://openshift.redhat.com/app/console/application_types*).

Another good website to help you find ready-made applications and app components is the OO-Index. Its sole purpose is to index OpenShift cartridges and QuickStarts.It was in active development at the time of this writing and the production URL was not yet known, but you should be able to find the link at OpenShift's website (*http://www.openshift.com*).

Given that a lot of cartridge code is hosted on GitHub, another way of finding a cartridge or QuickStart for a particular technology is to search for OpenShift (*https://github.com/search?q=openshift*) and the technology name on the GitHub website. Search engine results may also help you to unearth treasures, especially if the programmers have written blog posts about their work.

 If you cannot find an existing cartridge or QuickStart for the programming language, framework, or other technology you want to run on OpenShift, it does not mean all hope is lost. Most things that can run on Red Hat Enterprise Linux can run on OpenShift. You may be able to use the DIY cartridge (*https://www.openshift.com/developers/do-it-yourself*) (available via `rhc app create`) and install the technology manually. For example, Steve has written a blog post (*http://bit.ly/OPVFxU*) on how to run Minecraft on OpenShift. Alternatively, you could create your own cartridge (*http://bit.ly/1qCuZ2o*). Demonstrating how to create cartridges is beyond the scope of this book.

Popular downloadable cartridges and QuickStarts include:

- ActiveMQ (*http://github.com/bdecoste/openshift-origin-cartridge-activemq*)
- Django (*https://www.openshift.com/quickstarts/django*)
- Drupal (*https://www.openshift.com/quickstarts/drupal-8*)
- Flask (*https://github.com/openshift/flask-example*)

- Ghost (*https://www.openshift.com/quickstarts/ghost-on-openshift*)
- Go (*https://github.com/smarterclayton/openshift-go-cart*)
- Jekyll (*https://www.openshift.com/quickstarts/jekyll*)
- Rails (*https://github.com/openshift/rails-example*)
- Redis (*https://github.com/smarterclayton/openshift-redis-cart*)
- Spring (*https://www.openshift.com/quickstarts/spring-framework-on-jboss-eap6*)
- Vert.x (*https://github.com/vert-x/openshift-cartridge/*)
- WordPress (*https://www.openshift.com/quickstarts/wordpress-3x*)

Adding Third-Party Cartridges

To add a third-party cartridge to your application, you need to provide RHC with the URL to its manifest file, which will be called *manifest.yml*. This file is found within the *metadata* directory in the cartridge source repository. You can use this URL in RHC commands instead of a cartridge type such as *python-3.3* or *postgresql-9.2*; it can be used with the `rhc app create` and `rhc cartridge add` commands.

For example, to add the Monit cartridge mentioned in "Metrics and Monitoring" on page 31 to our Insult App application, we could use the following command (alternatively, we could use the shorter version (*http://goo.gl/eGL2Bs*) that redirects to the manifest URL, which the cartridge author provided in the documentation):

```
[me@localhost ~/insultapp]$ rhc cartridge add https://raw2.github.com/mfojtik/
openshift-origin-cartridge-monit/master/metadata/manifest.yml
The cartridge 'https://raw2.github.com/mfojtik/openshift-origin-cartridge-monit/
master/metadata/manifest.yml' will be downloaded and installed
Adding https://raw2.github.com/mfojtik/openshift-origin-cartridge-monit/master/
metadata/manifest.yml to application 'insultapp' ... done

mfojtik-monit-5.6 (monit 5.6)
-----------------------------
  From:  https://raw2.github.com/mfojtik/openshift-origin-cartridge-monit/master/
  metadata/manifest.yml
  Gears: Located with python-2.7, postgresql-9.2, cron-1.4

Please set the email you want to receive monit alerts:

$ rhc env set MONIT_ALERT_EMAIL=email@address.com -a insultapp
$ rhc cartridge restart monit -a insultapp

Monit Server Manager is running at: https://insultapp-osbeginnerbook.rhcloud.com/
monit-status
Username: admin
Password: Ny4nc=pt
```

```
You can add custom monitoring rules by editing ~/.monitrc file
```

 Unlike the supported cartridges maintained by OpenShift, community cartridges do not receive automatic security updates and upgrades.

If we later wish to remove the cartridge, we can reference it with the short name provided, as shown here:

```
[me@localhost ~/insultapp]$ rhc cartridge remove mfojtik-monit-5.6
Removing a cartridge is a destructive operation that may result in loss of data
associated with the cartridge.

Are you sure you wish to remove mfojtik-monit-5.6 from 'insultapp'? (yes|no):
yes

Removing mfojtik-monit-5.6 from 'insultapp' ... removed
```

In this chapter, we have seen how to go beyond the required web cartridge to add extra components to an OpenShift application. Additional cartridges can be used to provide databases, metrics and monitoring, job scheduling, and other useful capabilities. OpenShift Online provides a suite of supported cartridges that receive automatic updates; however, there are also an array of partner-provided and community cartridges and QuickStart applications available. Furthermore, developers can create their own cartridges to bring new technologies to OpenShift; the Cartridge Developer's Guide (*http:// bit.ly/1qCuZ2o*) details how to do so.

In the next chapter, we will show how to perform a mixed bag of tasks for managing your OpenShift application, such as accessing your gears and database via SSH, viewing the logs, and setting environment variables.

## CHAPTER 5

Environment and Application Management

Once you have added the application cartridges you need and pushed your code to the cloud, you will hopefully hit the OpenShift URL and find your app just works. Now is the time to throw your hands in the air and do a happy dance; this is the awesomesauce of Platform as a Service. Once you are all danced out, you might realize there are some aspects of your application you would like to explore further or tweak; the next few pages will help with that.

In this chapter, you will learn how to access your application's container, view its log output, and fiddle with its configuration should the need arise. We will explain how to connect to your application's gear via SSH, how to view and set OpenShift environment variables, and how to access application logs. We will also show how to make configuration changes to your application server or database and how to use marker files to set options such as hot deployment.

SSH Access

Your application's remote container, called a *gear*, can be accessed using the Secure Shell (SSH) protocol in the same way as you access regular machines. To communicate with OpenShift securely, your OpenShift account must first contain an SSH public key belonging to the machine from which you wish to connect. This key is uploaded to OpenShift when you first run the terminal command `rhc setup` (see Chapter 2 for more on this); you can also add keys manually via the OpenShift Web Console's *Settings* section.

The simplest way to connect to an application gear is to go to the command line, change into the directory where your app was cloned locally, and enter the command `rhc ssh`. This will start an SSH session with your main application gear. If the local clone of your application repository is not linked to your OpenShift app in RHC (in which case you will receive an error message), or you wish to SSH from another directory, you should add the `-a` *appname* option, replacing *appname* with the name of your app.

If you would prefer to use an alternative tool for creating an SSH connection, you can view the SSH URL you will need for your main application gear with the command rhc app show -a *appname*.

If your app is scalable and you would like to SSH into the other gears, you can use the command rhc app show --gears -a *appname* to view their SSH URLs and the ssh command-line tool to connect (e.g., ssh *user@host*).

Once you have connected to the gear via SSH, you will see a "Welcome to OpenShift console" message and a warning about making destructive modifications to your application; you should always take care when making changes on the gear directly as it is possible to make persistent, unversioned changes to your app and its environment. By default, you will find yourself in the home directory of the OpenShift user for your application, which will have a UUID username that doesn't quite roll off the tongue. If you list the contents of the directory, you will see subdirectories for the cartridges on your gear, as well as Git, your app's deployment history, and the app itself.

Here is the output from a sample SSH session with our Python demo application. We connect to the application gear, then use the ls command to list the contents of some of the key directories, starting with our OpenShift application user's home directory:

```
[me@localhost ~/insultapp]$ rhc ssh
Connecting to 6e7672676e61676976757570@insultapp-osbeginnerbook.rhcloud.com ...

*********************************************************************

You are accessing a service that is for use only by authorized users.
If you do not have authorization, discontinue use at once.
Any use of the services is subject to the applicable terms of the
agreement which can be found at:
https://www.openshift.com/legal

*********************************************************************

Welcome to OpenShift console

This console will assist you in managing OpenShift applications.

!!! IMPORTANT !!! IMPORTANT !!! IMPORTANT !!!
Shell access is quite powerful and it is possible for you to
accidentally damage your application.  Proceed with care!
If worse comes to worst, destroy your application with "rhc app delete"
and recreate it
!!! IMPORTANT !!! IMPORTANT !!! IMPORTANT !!!

Type "help" for more info.


[insultapp-osbeginnerbook.rhcloud.com 6e7672676e61676976757570]\> ls
app-deployments  app-root  cron  git  postgresql  python
```

```
[insultapp-osbeginnerbook.rhcloud.com 6e7672676e61676976757570]\> ls app-root
build-dependencies  data  dependencies  repo  runtime
[insultapp-osbeginnerbook.rhcloud.com 6e7672676e61676976757570]\> ls app-root
/repo
app.py.disabled  data  Insult_App.egg-info  libs  README.md  setup.py  setup.pyc
setup.pyo  wsgi
```

The demo application uses a Python cartridge, so there is a Python directory in the application's home directory. The *app-root* directory contains several important application subdirectories, notably *repo*, containing the current clone of the application's Git repository, and *data*, which is a persistent directory you will read more about later in the book (see Chapter 8).

When accessing an application gear via SSH, you can run the usual Linux commands you might execute on a local machine. However, there are some restrictions. Your app runs within a container secured with SELinux, and you do not have root access. As you would expect, you cannot access other applications running on the same remote machine. If you receive "Permission Denied" errors, it is likely because you have attempted to overstep your bounds. Remember, you are a developer, *not* an administrator on your gear.

Using SSH to Interact with a Database

One set of useful commands you can run when connected to an application gear via SSH are those associated with your database cartridge. If you are using PostgreSQL, as we are in our demo application, you can access your application database from your SSH session with the psql command. In the following example, we connect to the database, issue the help command to see what options are available, and then use \q to quit:

```
[insultapp-osbeginnerbook.rhcloud.com 6e7672676e61676976757570]\> psql
psql (9.2.4)
Type "help" for help.

insultapp=# help
You are using psql, the command-line interface to PostgreSQL.
Type:  \copyright for distribution terms
       \h for help with SQL commands
       \? for help with psql commands
       \g or terminate with semicolon to execute query
       \q to quit
insultapp=# \q
[insultapp-osbeginnerbook.rhcloud.com 6e7672676e61676976757570]\>
```

The OpenShift environment has been configured so that psql connects using the admin username and password to the default database. You can always override these options using the normal methods you use with psql. You may also like to use other PostgreSQL commands such as `pg_dump` or `pg_restore`. If you are using MySQL, you may wish to run commands, such as `mysql` and `mysqldump`, or, for MongoDB, `mongo` and `mongodump`.

Importing SQL in an SSH Session

The ability to issue database commands in an SSH session provides one method of importing data into your OpenShift database. You can connect to the database and enter SQL manually if you want to test it out or edit something specific. Most times, though, you will want to import your data from a file.

One way you can transfer a SQL file to your database gear is to use the `scp` (secure copy) command. Here is an example of sending a file called *import.sql* to the persistent *data* directory on our example application gear. You can use the command `rhc app show --gears` to obtain the SSH URL of the gear:

```
[me@localhost ~/insultapp]$ scp import.sql 6e7672676e61676976757570@insultapp
-osbeginnerbook.rhcloud.com:~/app-root/data
import.sql                                    100% 5360      8.2KB/s   00:00
```

If your database cartridge shares a gear with your application cartridge, which it will if your app is not scalable, another way of copying your SQL file to your gear is to check it in to your Git repository. For our Insult App, we have added, committed, and pushed an *import.sql* file at the root level of the repository. It contains the full list of Shakespearean insults, split into nouns and adjectives. You can view the full contents of this file in the book's Git repository (see "Using Code Examples" on page xi). Here is an excerpt:

```
DROP TABLE IF EXISTS short_adjective;
DROP TABLE IF EXISTS long_adjective;
DROP TABLE IF EXISTS noun;

BEGIN;

CREATE TABLE short_adjective (id serial PRIMARY KEY, string varchar);
CREATE TABLE long_adjective (id serial PRIMARY KEY, string varchar);
CREATE TABLE noun (id serial PRIMARY KEY, string varchar);

INSERT INTO short_adjective (string) VALUES ('artless');
INSERT INTO short_adjective (string) VALUES ('bawdy');
INSERT INTO short_adjective (string) VALUES ('beslubbering');

INSERT INTO long_adjective (string) VALUES ('base-court');
INSERT INTO long_adjective (string) VALUES ('bat-fowling');
INSERT INTO long_adjective (string) VALUES ('beef-witted');

INSERT INTO noun (string) VALUES ('apple-john');
INSERT INTO noun (string) VALUES ('baggage');
INSERT INTO noun (string) VALUES ('barnacle');
```

To import this data into our PostgreSQL database, we issue the following commands within an SSH session:

```
[insultapp-osbeginnerbook.rhcloud.com 6e7672676e61676976757570]\> cd app-root
/repo/
[insultapp-osbeginnerbook.rhcloud.com repo]\> psql -f import.sql
```

Our example application database is now populated and ready to help produce a bundle of new insults; we will alter our code to make use of this in the next chapter.

 Executing database commands in an SSH session is not the only method of connecting to your app database; we will demonstrate how to connect via your app code in Chapter 6 and how to use port forwarding to facilitate access in Chapter 7.

Environment Variables

Only masochistic developers hardcode database connection strings or server ports; we have environment variables to save us from the pain of marrying code to a particular environment. OpenShift and its standard cartridges have a bunch of useful environment variables available out of the box that you can reference in your applications. It is also possible to set custom environment variables.

 Due to some maintenance that the operations team may need to do, your application's IP address can change. Hardcoding the values pointed to by the environment variables in your OpenShift application can cause it to break. So, in case you didn't get the message, don't hardcode the values of the environment variables.

You can view the values of some of the essential environment variables, such as your database details, in the output of the command rhc app show -a *appname*. To view all of the environment variables and their values, SSH into your application gear and execute the command env. To view only the environment variables with names including the word "OPENSHIFT," use the command env | grep OPENSHIFT.

Preconfigured Environment Variables

Table 5-1 outlines some of the key preconfigured environment variables for our demo application. Other cartridges have similar variables: just replace PYTHON or POSTGRESQL with the relevant cartridge or database name.

Table 5-1. Useful environment variables

Environment variable	Value	Purpose
OPENSHIFT_APP_NAME	insultapp	Application name
OPENSHIFT_APP_DNS	insultapp-osbeginnerbook.rhcloud.com	Application domain name
OPENSHIFT_PYTHON_IP	19.66.2.6	IP address the app listens on
OPENSHIFT_PYTHON_PORT	8080	Port the app receives external requests on
OPENSHIFT_SECRET_TOKEN	Not shown for brevity	128-character string unique to the application and synced across all gears
OPENSHIFT_DATA_DIR	$OPENSHIFT_HOMEDIR/app-root/data/	Persistent data directory
OPENSHIFT_REPO_DIR	$OPENSHIFT_HOMEDIR/app-root/runtime/repo/	Currently deployed copy of the app
OPENSHIFT_TMP_DIR	/tmp/	Temporary directory; SELinux and PAM namespaces protect data from other users
OPENSHIFT_PYTHON_LOG_DIR	$OPENSHIFT_HOMEDIR/python/logs/	Cartridge-specific log directory
OPENSHIFT_POST GRESQL_DB_LOG_DIR	$OPENSHIFT_HOMEDIR/post gresql/log/	Database log directory
OPENSHIFT_POSTGRESQL_DB_HOST	19.66.2.7	Database hostname or IP
OPENSHIFT_POSTGRESQL_DB_PORT	5432	Database port
OPENSHIFT_POSTGRESQL_DB_USER NAME	adminm4rvN42	Database username
OPENSHIFT_POSTGRESQL_DB_PASS WORD	SLat4aTfsSt1	Database password

Custom Environment Variables

Developers can extend the array of built-in environment variables by adding their own. One way to achieve this is to export the custom variables in one of the action hook scripts that runs before your application starts. For example, you could add the line export FOO=bar to *.openshift/action_hooks/pre_start_python*. Alternatively, you can create and set custom environment variables with RHC. This is the preferred solution if the values of your environment variables are sensitive and hence you would rather not check them in to your Git repository.

Custom environment variables can be managed with the RHC commands env set, env list, env show, and env unset. Here is an example of each command:

```
[me@localhost ~]$ rhc env set API_USERNAME=admin API_PASSWORD=secret -a
insultapp
Setting environment variable(s) ... done
[me@localhost ~]$ rhc env list -a insultapp
API_PASSWORD=secret
API_USERNAME=admin
[me@localhost ~]$ rhc unset API_PASSWORD -a insultapp
Removing environment variables is a destructive operation that may result in
loss of data.
API_PASSWORD

Are you sure you wish to remove the environment variable(s) above from
application 'insultapp'? (yes|no): yes

Removing environment variable(s) ... removed
[me@localhost ~]$ rhc env show API_USERNAME API_PASSWORD -a insultapp
API_USERNAME=admin
```

Overriding Preconfigured Environment Variables

Some preconfigured environment variables can be overridden: for example, OPEN
SHIFT_SECRET_TOKEN. This environment variable provides a random token string that
is synchronized across gears. Example uses for this include cookie encryption, forming
JBoss clusters, and seeding a Rails secret token. The OPENSHIFT_SECRET_TOKEN variable
is set by default with a random value generated when the application is created. However,
it can be overridden with RHC if you wish to replace it with a secret string you have
generated yourself:

```
[me@localhost ~/insultapp]$ rhc env set OPENSHIFT_SECRET_TOKEN=new_token
Setting environment variable(s) ... done
```

You can override other preconfigured environment variables in the same fashion. These
will then be listed alongside your custom variables when you run the command rhc
env list. Some preconfigured environment variables are protected and cannot be
overridden; you will receive an error message if you attempt to override one of these
with RHC.

Log Access

To ensure your application is working correctly, or troubleshoot when it is not, you may
want to view the log files. You can do this by connecting to the application gear via SSH
and navigating to the relevant locations, which you can find by checking the environment variables as described in the previous section. In general, you will find the log
directories for web cartridges can be referenced with $OPENSHIFT_<car-
tridge>_LOG_DIR and databases with $OPENSHIFT_<database>_DB_LOG_DIR. For
example, our demo application's logs are directed to $OPEN-
SHIFT_PYTHON_LOG_DIR and $OPENSHIFT_POSTGRESQL_DB_LOG_DIR.

A simpler method for checking the logs is to use RHC's `tail` command. By default, `rhc tail -a` *appname* will tail the log files within the cartridges' log directories; in the case of our Python application, this means the files stored in *$OPENSHIFT_HOMEDIR/python/logs* and *$OPENSHIFT_HOMEDIR_postgresql/log*. However, you can specify a different or more specific set of files, relative to *$OPENSHIFT_HOMEDIR*, with the `-f` option. You can also set various Linux `tail` command options by adding `-o`.

The following command tails the `insultapp` application's database logs only, outputting the last 50 lines rather than the default of the last 10:

```
[me@localhost ~]$ rhc tail -f postgresql/log/* -o '-n 50' -a insultapp
```

Application and database cartridges will be configured to output their logs to the directories referenced by the aforementioned environment variables by default. If you produce application-specific logs, you should direct these to your web cartridge's log directory as well, e.g., *$OPENSHIFT_PYTHON_LOG_DIR*. Files in this directory will automatically be included in the output of the `rhc tail` command.

To learn how to manage disk usage and back up your remote files, including log files, see Chapters 8 and 9.

Changing Application Server or Database Settings

One of the advantages of using a Platform as a Service is that you do not have to tinker with dozens of configuration files just to get an app running in the cloud. That said, you may well want to alter the out-of-the-box config, and many cartridges facilitate that.

Application Server Configuration Changes

If you are coding in Java and using an application server such as Tomcat, JBoss, or WildFly, you can override server config files within your OpenShift Git repository. This is where you could change, for example, the application server's log levels or settings for your data source. Look inside the *.openshift/config* directory to see which files have been cloned ready for modification. These configuration files will already include the relevant OpenShift environment variables, so you will want to use them as a starting point when making changes.

Many of the other application cartridges are Apache-based. You cannot edit the main *httpd.conf* file, but some cartridges do offer configuration options. One way to make Apache configuration changes to individual directories is by using *.htaccess* files. A common use case for this is adding an *.htaccess* file containing *mod_rewrite* directives to the */php* directory in a WordPress application, so requests to the default OpenShift URL are redirected to a custom domain. For specific configuration options for your cartridge of interest, please refer to its documentation.

Database Configuration Changes

Another set of cartridges users may wish to reconfigure are the database cartridges. For example, you may want to change the log rotation frequency or tweak settings for resource usage or caching. If you need to change PostgreSQL's configuration, you can edit the *postgresql.conf* file. If your application is not scalable, you can do this by using SSH to connect to your app gear, navigating to *$OPENSHIFT_HOMEDIR/postgresql/conf*, and opening the file with Vim, Nano, or some other editor. If your application is scalable, the PostgreSQL instance will have its own gear; use the command `rhc app show --gears -a` *appname* to view its SSH URL, then connect to the database gear with the `ssh` command (or your preferred SSH tool). The *postgresql.conf* file will be in the same location as on an application gear with an embedded PostgreSQL cartridge. Once you have made your changes, you can restart the PostgreSQL cartridge so that they take effect with the command `rhc cartridge restart postgresql -a` *appname*.

The general process for making config changes to other database cartridges is the same as described for PostgreSQL. In the case of MySQL, the relevant config file can be found at *$OPENSHIFT_HOMEDIR/mysql/conf/my.cnf*. The MongoDB config file is available at *$OPENSHIFT_HOMEDIR/mongodb/conf/mongodb.conf*.

Using Marker Files

Many basic OpenShift cartridge configuration options are controlled with marker files. If a particular marker file is present, the option is enabled; otherwise, the default behavior prevails. Marker files are added in an OpenShift application's Git repository, in the *.openshift/markers* directory. The contents of marker files are irrelevant; they are empty files. They do not have any file extension.

One of the most common marker files used is *hot_deploy*—as mentioned in "Hot-Deploying Code" on page 22—which tells OpenShift to deploy new builds without restarting the cartridge server. Other marker files you may be interested in include *force_clean_build* (instructs OpenShift to remove previously built artifacts before building the app), *disable_auto_scaling* (prevents scalable applications from scaling according to load), and *java7* (if this is removed, Java cartridges will use Java 6).

The marker files must be committed and pushed with Git. Here is an example of adding the *force_clean_build* marker to our example app:

```
[me@localhost ~/insultapp]$ touch .openshift/markers/force_clean_build
[me@localhost ~/insultapp]$ git add .openshift/markers/force_clean_build
[me@localhost ~/insultapp]$ git commit -m "Adding marker to force clean build"
[me@localhost ~/insultapp]$ git push
```

This will cause OpenShift to re-create the app's virtual environment and reinstall the required Python eggs (these are code bundles, like JARs in Java). We do not want this to happen on every build as it takes time to download those dependencies, so once we are satisfied that the environment is clean we would remove the marker file.

It's time to take a deep breath; we have learned a lot in this chapter. We showed how to use SSH to connect to your application's gears and interact with databases hosted on OpenShift. We know that application configuration is easier to maintain when we use environment variables rather than hardcoded values; in this chapter we learned how to access the values of OpenShift's environment vars and how to define our own. We discussed OpenShift application log access with `rhc tail` and where to direct app log output. Finally, we explained how to make application server and database configuration changes and how to control app config switches with marker files.

In the next chapter, we will dive into application dependencies and show how to connect to a database from your OpenShift app code.

## CHAPTER 6

Library Dependencies

All applications beyond the very simple will have a requirement to use outside libraries or dependencies. Examples of dependencies might be libraries for database connectivity, turning images to text (object character recognition or OCR), calculating statistics, or web templating. In this chapter we will show you how to use libraries in your OpenShift applications. We will add the database drivers to our Insult App and then use it to access the insults stored in the database.

Where to Declare Dependencies

All modern programming languages have a "build" process; OpenShift takes advantage of this to build your application dependencies. At the time of this writing we are using the processes listed in Table 6-1 to pull in dependencies for external libraries.

Table 6-1. Dependency mechanisms used by OpenShift, by language

Language	Dependency mechanism
Java	Maven (*http://maven.apache.org/*)
Python	Pip (*http://www.pip-installer.org/en/latest/*)
Ruby	Gem (*http://rubygems.org/*)
Node.js (JavaScript)	NPM (*https://npmjs.org/*)
PHP	Pear (*http://pear.php.net/*)
Perl	CPAN (*http://www.cpan.org/*)

We have tried to make the process as close to development on your local machine as possible. So, for example, with Python if you wanted to download the "default" Post-greSQL drivers (*psycopg2*) to your local machine you would use Pip:

```
$ pip install psycopg2
```

This would install the Psycopg2 drivers to a location where Python can see them on your local machine. The way to reproduce this functionality on OpenShift is to include the dependency in the appropriate "application metadata" file. When you include your dependencies in this file, OpenShift will notice the dependencies during the build process and then download the files and put them where your language runtime can see them. Table 6-2 presents a listing of all the files for a variety of languages.

Table 6-2. Files used for dependency declaration

Language	Dependency file
Java	*pom.xml*
Python	*setup.py/requirements.txt*
Ruby	*Gemfile.lock*
Node.js (JavaScript)	*package.json*
PHP	*deplist.txt*
Perl	*deplist.txt*

Let's go ahead and add Psycopg2 to our project so we can use the library to connect to our database of insults. Go into your local Git repository and edit the *setup.py* file. We already have a dependency declaration for Flask (see "Modifying Application Code" on page 18), and now we are going to add one for Psycopg2. Your install dependencies section should look like this now:

```
install_requires=['Flask==0.10.1', 'psycopg2==2.5.2'],
```

The best practice on OpenShift is to always specify an exact version number for your dependencies. There are two reasons why:

1. If you use >= the build process will always have to check to see if there is a newer version of the library available than what is currently installed. This will slow down your build process.

2. There is the possibility that there will be a new version of the library that is incompatible with your code. Not explicitly stating a specific version number could lead to your application breaking when you don't expect it.

The first time you git push with this new dependency, the build will take longer because of the download and build of the new dependency. After that OpenShift will use the cached version. This is particularly noticeable for Java developers with Maven builds, since the default *pom.xml* requires the full JEE dependency.

When you do your git push, you should see something like the following in the output:

```
...
remote: Processing dependencies for Insult-App==1.0
remote: Searching for psycopg2==2.5.2
remote: Best match: psycopg2 2.5.2
remote: Processing psycopg2-2.5.2-py2.7-linux-x86_64.egg
...
```

These are the lines where the OpenShift build process is adding the Psycopg2 library to
the virtual environment for your application.

 A common problem we see in the forums goes something like: "The
application works fine on my local machine but when I deploy to
OpenShift I get an error that *LibraryX* is not available." This is usually a sign that you have not declared your dependency in the proper file or with the proper syntax for OpenShift to download it and
make it available. Unless it is in your Git repository or declared as a
dependency in the proper file, it will not be available to your application code.

Incorporating Your Own Binary Dependencies

For each programming language, there is a designated location in the Git repository
where you can place your own binaries for your application and have the build pick
them up (Table 6-3). For example, you would do this if you have a binary library that
you use within your company that you do not want to put in a public repository or in
the code base. This way you can reuse the library without exposing the code.

Table 6-3. Location to place your own libraries

Language	Location in repository for binaries
Java	More complicated as they have to be part of Maven; please see OpenShift knowledge base article E1040 (*http://bit.ly/1gwrLp5*). The other option is to bundle all the libs in your WAR file and just deploy the WAR.
Python	*libs*
Ruby	*[role="filename"]vendor/cache/{myfile}.gem*
Node.js (JavaScript)	*node_modules*
PHP	*libs*
Perl	*libs*

Placing your libraries in these locations means you can use your own libraries, ensure
a certain version of a library is used, or include nonpublic libraries.

Some of these languages also have the ability to point to a library in a different Git
repository or in other places "on disk." For example, in your Ruby application you can
specify the location to your Gem in your *Gemfile.lock* file. This is a much more flexible
method than using the location specified earlier. The same holds with *setup.py* or

requirements.txt for Python; your metadata file can point to a GitHub repository or other publicly accessible locations.

Modifying Your Application to Use the Database

Now that we know how to pull in dependencies, let's go ahead and modify our code to take advantage of the database. We are going to design the application so that our insult propagation crew can search out new insults, add them to the database, and have them appear without any code changes. We designed the database tables so we could pick from each adjective type and noun separately and add to each group separately.

We did such a nice job with the separation of concerns between our classes in our original application that we only have to modify *insulter.py*. We are going to replace the static lists of adjectives and nouns with calls to the database, but nothing else in the application has to change. Even within *insulter.py* we only have to modify one method. Hooray for clean code!

One quick note before we dig in: as much as we would like to believe Insult App will be hugely successful and allow us to retire early, this app will probably have only one or two users at a time (if we are lucky). Therefore, we are not going to add the overhead of having a connection pool for the database connections. Given that database connections take a relatively long time to establish, in any real production application you would want to use a connection pool for your database connections.

All right, on to the code!

Code to Connect to the Database

Since WSGI acts like CGI, where each class is spun up and run each time there is a request, we are just going to go ahead and create a method to open a database connection and then call it in the function where we retrieve the words to be used. Using Pyscopg2 is incredibly easy, and the environment variables put in by OpenShift allow us to establish the connection in a portable way. First, we define a method to get a *cursor* (the basic object that does all the database interaction). Here is the excerpt from *insulter.py*:

```
import psycopg2
...


def get_cursor():
    #open a connection
    conn = psycopg2.connect(database=os.environ['OPENSHIFT_APP_NAME'],
                    user=os.environ['OPENSHIFT_POSTGRESQL_DB_USERNAME'],
                    password=os.environ['OPENSHIFT_POSTGRESQL_DB_PASSWORD'],
                    host=os.environ['OPENSHIFT_POSTGRESQL_DB_HOST'],
                    port=os.environ['OPENSHIFT_POSTGRESQL_DB_PORT'] )
    #get a cursor from the connection
```

```
cursor = conn.cursor()
return cursor
```

While it is bad form even in noncloud applications to hardcode database connection parameters, in cloud applications it also has the potential to break your application. If, for some reason, operations needs to migrate your gear to a different set of servers and the IP addresses change, your application will still work if you used environment variables. The other benefit to using environment variables is that you can give your Git repository to another developer, who can push the code into his own version of the application, and it will just work because the environment variables in his version will point to the new information.

Code to Close the Database Connection

Whenever you open a database connection you eventually have to close it, or your application will ultimately stop working because you have used up all the connections. If you use a database pool, this can help with connection exhaustion, but as noted earlier, we are not using a pool. Here is the code from *insulter.py* to close the cursor:

```
def close_cursor(cursor):
    conn = cursor.connection
    cursor.close()
    conn.close()
```

Code to Query the Terms for the Insult

Now that we have a connection to the database, we need to query it for the words we want. Since we want to pick a word at random from the tables, we need to use a little bit of fancy SQL. We found an interesting solution to the problem on Stack Overflow (*http://bit.ly/1oTApSQ*) for PostgreSQL. The basic idea is you use the OFFSET (*http://bit.ly/1gq5UTZ*) modifier in the SQL query. Here is the description of the OFFSET keyword in the PostgreSQL manual:

> OFFSET says to skip that many rows before beginning to return rows… If both OFFSET and LIMIT appear, then OFFSET rows are skipped before starting to count the LIMIT rows that are returned.

We are basically just telling PostgreSQL to pick a random number between 1 and the total number of rows and use that as the offset for where to start returning results, and then just give us one result.

In the function, we pass in the cursor and the name of the table we want to execute the query against. Psycopg2 returns a Python tuple, so we just grab the first element in the tuple:

```
def get_word(cursor, table):
    sql = "select string from " + table + " offset random()*
    (select count(*) from " + table + ") limit 1;"
```

```
cursor.execute(sql)
result = cursor.fetchone()
return result[0]
```

Now that we have that function in place, we can basically replace all the lists and the random calls with just a simple set of calls to the get_word function. The flow now becomes open a cursor, make the calls, and then finally close the cursor—nice and simple:

```
def generate_insult():
    local_cursor = get_cursor()
    final_insult = get_word(local_cursor, "short_adjective") + " " +
     get_word(local_cursor, "long_adjective") + " " +
     get_word(local_cursor, "noun")
    close_cursor(local_cursor)
    return final_insult
```

What We Have Gained by Adding a Database

Now that we have changed over our application to use a database, we can add new terms without having to touch the code, build, and deploy. As a matter of fact, we could write a separate web page for people to add new terms and the insult page would pick them up on the fly. In this chapter, we have also learned how to add library dependencies to our projects on OpenShift, and finally, how to access a database in an OpenShift application. At this point our application is finished. From here on, we are going to talk more about how to interact and monitor the application behind the scenes.

## CHAPTER 7

Networking

Even though a PaaS abstracts away much of the networking complexity, there is still a lot you can do with the network on OpenShift. In this chapter we will cover some of the networking you can do to either make your work easier or add capabilities to your application.

WebSockets

One of the hot new technologies in web applications is the WebSocket protocol (*http://en.wikipedia.org/wiki/WebSocket*). WebSockets allow the client to open a persistent connection to the server. In this way, the server can push information to the client, rather than always having the client pull information from the server. This has a whole host of interesting applications and is much more efficient than using long polling, an alternative technique that simulates two-way communication. Examples of applications this could be used for include:

- Real-time chat applications
- Fleet or vehicle tracking, or any stream of positions
- Multiplayer gaming
- Monitoring applications
- Real-time auction sites

The prerequisites to using WebSockets are:

- Your server supports WebSockets. Some examples are:
  — Node.js (JavaScript)
  — Twisted (Python)
  — Socky (Ruby)

— Socket (PHP)

— Tomcat7, Netty, and Vert.x (Java and more)

- Using a browser that supports WebSockets, which appears to be all the current browsers (*http://caniuse.com/websockets*).

From there, the basic flow of using WebSockets in your application is:

- The client application makes an upgrade request from HTTP to the WebSocket protocol.
- The server responds that it supports the protocol.
- Away they go, talking over the WebSocket protocol rather than over HTTP.

Of course this is a simplification, but you get the basic idea. If you want to read a more complete tutorial of how it works there are plenty of good examples; Matt West has written a blog post (*http://bit.ly/1l9Muq6*) covering the basics.

At the time of writing, OpenShift provided support for WebSockets but only at a beta level. This means that it works but you have to use alternative ports to 80 to make your WebSocket connections. Specifically, the URL you use to open a WebSocket connection has to go to port 8000 for WS (standard WebSocket) or 8443 for WSS (secure Web-Socket). What this means in practice is that you cannot make your connection from the client like this:

```
//Standard WebSocket
var socket = new WebSocket('ws://insultapp-osbeginnerbook.rhcloud.com');

//Secure WebSocket
var socket = new WebSocket('wss://insultapp-osbeginnerbook.rhcloud.com');
```

Rather, you need to specify the port number:

```
//Standard WebSocket
var socket = new WebSocket('ws://insultapp-osbeginnerbook.rhcloud.com:8000');

//Secure WebSocket
var socket = new WebSocket('wss://insultapp-osbeginnerbook.rhcloud.com:8443');
```

Please note that when trying to use WebSockets with OpenShift you need to have a server that supports WebSockets. OpenShift currently uses Apache 2.2 to serve content for the default PHP, Python, Perl, and Ruby cartridges. This version of Apache does not support WebSockets, so for any of those languages you would have to create a DIY cartridge or your own language cartridge. Here is an example of an OpenShift DIY (*http://bit.ly/1rtEe5j*) that uses Python 2.6 with Tornado (a WebSocket-capable server). There is also an advanced Ruby cartridge (*http://bit.ly/PAjN8J*) that allows you to use Web-Sockets with Ruby. The only cartridges that support WebSockets out of the box are Node.js, Tomcat 7, and the WildFly 8 (*http://bit.ly/1qCEjDk*) Java application server. The version of the Apache HTTP server may change by the time you get this book, so please check on the OpenShift website for the latest information on WebSocket support.

Finally, each WebSocket connection you make to the server counts as a connection for the purposes of autoscaling of your application. Currently on OpenShift, when a scalable app has more than 16 connections on the gear it will trigger a scale-up event, causing OpenShift to spin up a new gear, install the application code on it, and plug it into the load balancer. That threshold includes any combination of HTTP and WebSocket connections.

SSH Port Forwarding

As explained in Chapter 1, all communication with your gear occurs over the Secure Shell (SSH) protocol. One of the great features of SSH is *port forwarding*, which allows you to securely communicate with your gear and make it appear as if the services on the gear are running on your own machine. The basic idea is that SSH takes ports on your local machines and tunnels them over a secure connection to a port on the remote machine. For example, you can use SSH to take port 9999 on your local machine and have it attach to port 5432 on your gear, which is the port that PostgreSQL listens on. Now when you connect to port 9999 on your local machine, all your traffic to that port will be sent directly to port 5432 on your gear.

Some potential uses of SSH port fowarding are:

- Attaching your database admin software on your local machine to the DB in your OpenShift application
- Desktop software such as Excel or QGIS directly using data on the server
- Having your code on your local machine work with the database in your OpenShift application

- Attaching the debugger on your local machine to the process running on OpenShift

To give an example, we are going to port forward for all the running servers on our gear and then connect from the local laptop to our PostgreSQL instance on the gear using the `psql` command-line tool. Even though `psql` will be running on our local machine, with access to local SQL files, it will actually be talking to the PostgreSQL instance on OpenShift. You could use this same technique to have a development web application on your local machine talking to your OpenShift PostgreSQL instance before you deploy the web application to OpenShift.

Before we begin, you are going to need your username and password for your OpenShift database. If you don't have this information written down, you can retrieve it with the `rhc show` command:

```
[me@localhost insultapp]$ rhc app show
insultapp @ http://insultapp-osbeginnerbook.rhcloud.com/
(uuid: 6e7672676e61676976757570)
--------------------------------------------------------------------------
  Domain:      osbeginnerbook
  Created:     Mar 14  1:59 PM
  Gears:       1 (defaults to small)
  Git URL:     ssh://6e7672676e61676976757570@insultapp-osbeginnerbook.rhcloud
  .com/~/git/insultapp.git/
  SSH:         6e7672676e61676976757570@insultapp-osbeginnerbook.rhcloud.com
  Deployment:  auto (on git push)

  python-2.7 (Python 2.7)
  ----------------------
    Gears: Located with postgresql-9.2, cron-1.4

  postgresql-9.2 (PostgreSQL 9.2)
  ------------------------------
    Gears:           Located with python-2.7, cron-1.4
    Connection URL:  postgresql://$OPENSHIFT_POSTGRESQL_DB_HOST:
    $OPENSHIFT_POSTGRESQL_DB_PORT
    Database Name:   insultapp
->  Password:        SLat4aTfsSt1
->  Username:        adminm4rvN42

  cron-1.4 (Cron 1.4)
  ------------------
    Gears: Located with python-2.7, postgresql-9.2
```

We marked the two lines containing the username and password with a ->. Make note of these because you will need to use them when you connect to your database.

Next we use the `rhc port-forward` command to have the command-line tools port forward all listening ports over SSH:

```
[me@localhost insultapp]$ rhc port-forward
Forwarding ports ...
Address already in use - bind(2) while forwarding port 5432. Trying
local port 5433

To connect to a service running on OpenShift, use the Local address

Service     Local               OpenShift
---------   ---------------- ---- ----------------
httpd       127.0.0.1:8080   =>  19.66.2.6:8080
postgresql 127.0.0.1:5433    =>  19.66.2.7:5432

Press CTRL-C to terminate port forwarding
```

You can see from this output that there is a local PostgreSQL server running bound to port 5432, forcing the port-forward command to bind to 5433. Now on a local machine, when we connect to the local loopback address (127.0.0.1) on port 5433 we will actually be connecting to PostgreSQL on the gear. Let's go ahead and connect:

```
[me@localhost insultapp]$ psql -h 127.0.0.1 -p 5433 -U adminm4rvN42 insultapp
Password for user adminm4rvN42:
psql (9.3.2, server 9.2.4)
Type "help" for help.

insultapp=# \dt
                List of relations
 Schema |       Name       | Type  |    Owner
--------+------------------+-------+--------------
 public | long_adjective   | table | adminm4rvN42
 public | noun             | table | adminm4rvN42
 public | short_adjective  | table | adminm4rvN42
(3 rows)

insultapp=#
```

There is no option to enter the password with the command, but it did prompt for one on the second line. We entered **SLat4aTfsSt1**, and then we were at the PostgreSQL command prompt talking to our server. We executed the \dt command, which lists all the tables in the database, just to show that we are actually talking to the database running on our gear.

Custom URLs

While it is convenient that OpenShift gives you a predefined URL that works out of the box, you may want to use your own URL. This is actually quite easy to accomplish on OpenShift. Before we get to that, though we need to understand a little about DNS names. There are at least two types of DNS records that deal with URLs—*A records* and

CNAME records. An A record can reference any URL, such as *insultapp.com* or *www.insultapp.com*, and can take this name and point it at an IP address, like Red Hat does with *redhat.com*, which points to 10.4.127.150. You have to have an IP address to be able to use an A record. The benefit of an A record is that you can use the root or apex name for your web application, such as *http://insultapp.com*.

CNAME records are used to take one name, such as *www.insultapp.com*, and point it to a canonical (authoritative) name, such as *insultapp-osbeginnerbook.rhcloud.com*. For all your OpenShift applications, the URL provided by default when you create your application is the canonical URL. You would use CNAME records where a provider doesn't actually give you an IP address; this usually occurs with a *content delivery network* (CDN) such as Akamai or Edgenet, or with a PaaS such as OpenShift. The drawback to CNAME records is that they can never map a root record to another name. For example, you cannot take *insultapp.com* and point it to *insultapp-osbeginnerbook.rhcloud.com*. This has nothing to do with the limitations of OpenShift or your CDN—this is per Internet Engineering Task Force (IETF) specifications.

One of the most frequent questions we get, given this restriction, is, "How do I get *insultapp.com* to point to *insultapp-osbeginnerbook.rhcloud.com*?" There are several ways to do this, each with its own trade-offs, but we are going to cover the most common method—using an HTTP redirect to handle getting the user to your web application. With some DNS providers this is called "naked domain hosting." Let's cover the basic idea with Insult App:

1. Go to your DNS provider and make a CNAME record to point *www.insultapp.com* to *insultapp-osbeginnerbook.rhcloud.com*.

2. Do an HTTP redirect from *insultapp.com* to *www.insultapp.com*. This can be achieved by:

    a. Hosting your own web server and placing a redirect as the response page at *http://insultapp.com*.

    b. Finding a DNS provider that does naked domain hosting (also called apex domain hosting). In this case the DNS provider runs a web server for you and does the redirect on its servers.

To finish up the whole custom URL process you need to go to your command-line tools or the Web Console and define what URLs you have pointed to the canonical URL on OpenShift. The process is as simple as:

```
$ rhc alias add <application> <alias>
```

For our example, you would enter:

```
$ rhc alias add insultapp www.insultapp.com
```

Since this is a very frequently asked question, we are going to list the steps one more time for the whole process:

1. Purchase a DNS name.

2. Register a CNAME record with your DNS provider that points a subdomain you just bought (e.g., *www.abc.com*) to the canonical URL you got from OpenShift.

3. If you want to point to a primary domain, make sure your DNS provider offers naked domain hosting and point your primary domain at the canonical URL.

4. Finally, register each URL for which you created a CNAME with an OpenShift alias.

 Although you may be tempted to take the IP address that comes back when you do a `dig` or `nslookup` on your OpenShift URL and use it for your A record, resist! OpenShift may change the IP address for your app as part of normal maintenance or other operations. When this happens your DNS entry will be wrong and nobody will be able to get to your site using the A record URL, turning you into a sad panda. Nobody likes a sad panda, so don't do it.

SSL Certificates

Another common request from developers is to use HTTPS with their applications. By default, all applications on OpenShift can piggyback off the certificate provided for free. OpenShift Online provides a valid certificate for all **.rhcloud.com* URLs. This means that if we wanted to point users to *https://insultapp-osbeginnerbook.rhcloud.com*, the SSL certificate would be valid and the browser would show the connection as SSL secured.

However, as we discussed earlier, you may want to use your own domain name on OpenShift. In this case, the browser would see the URL as *https://www.insultapp.com* but the certificate would only be valid for **.rhcloud.com* URLs, causing the browser to alert the user that there was something wrong with the HTTPS session. The traffic would still be encrypted and the data secure, but the user would see an error with the HTTPS session.

OpenShift provides the ability for you to add your own SSL certs that match the custom domain names. This capability is provided when you enter the paid tier (*https://www.openshift.com/products/pricing*). At that level of service, you can add your own certificates and private key files for any aliases you have.

We are going to assume you have already obtained a Base64 PEM-encoded certificate file (it usually has a *.crt* or *.pem* extension). Be sure to obtain a file from a legitimate certificate provider with a signature recognized by most browsers, to avoid warning pop-ups. The private keys to go with the certificate must be in a separate file. If the private key is encrypted you will also need to have the password available.

Once you have all that in hand you can use the RHC command-line tools to upload the certificates. The general form of the command is:

```
rhc alias update-cert application alias --certificate mycert.pem
--private-key myprivatekey
```

The reason you have to give both the application and the alias is that an application may have multiple aliases, each of which would require its own cert. From then on, whenever a user hits your web application with an HTTPS URL and one of your aliases, there will be no error in the browser.

Please note that at the time of writing, the custom certificates will not work with the OpenShift secure WebSocket solution. In this situation, the browser will show an error for a secure WebSocket and the user will have to manually accept the certificate.

Talking to Other Services

While there are a lot of services provided out of the box with OpenShift, it also has a robust partner ecosystem (*https://www.openshift.com/partners*) for adding even more functionality to your application. You can add things such as caching solutions, monitoring solutions, Mobile Backend as a Service (MBaaS), or Big Data as a Service (BDaaS). One of the services most commonly used with OpenShift is an email service such as SendGrid. Given that the Online servers are hosted on Amazon Web Services, any email sent from the servers will be coming from an Amazon IP, which are blacklisted by most SMTP servers. For this reason, quite a few OpenShift users use SendGrid to send email in their applications.

For example, if we wanted to send insults to people through our app (which would probably break a whole bunch of spam laws), we could do it using this service. Since we like our freedom, we will only talk you through how you would use the service in our application. Since it is so simple, there is actually not much to say: you would just add code like the example SendGrid Python snippet (*http://sendgrid.com/docs/Code_Exam ples/python.html*). In that snippet, you are using the SendGrid SMTP servers just like you would use any other SMTP server. There are also examples on that page showing how to use the SendGrid Python library and the SendGrid web APIs to send emails.

We could also use a service for in-application analytics such as Keen IO (*https:// keen.io*). It basically lets you send arbitrary JSON to its service, store it, and use an API to analyze it, and then gives you a nice JavaScript API to make visualizations using your data. It has a full set of docs (*https://keen.io/docs/*) and a simple Python API (*https:// github.com/keenlabs/KeenClient-Python*). By using a partner like this with OpenShift, you can quickly add new functionality without having to learn it all from scratch. This gives you more time to focus on making your application usable and awesome. Don't forget to see "Environment Variables" on page 41 for the preferred method for storing your API key or username and password using the rhc env command.

Addressable Ports

Some OpenShift partner services, other services you might want to use, or other external servers you want to connect to may not talk over HTTP or another standard port like 25 (for SMTP). In these cases, such as when talking to an IRC server, you need to make sure you can connect from your OpenShift gear on an outbound port to your desired external endpoint. OpenShift uses SELinux to control the ability of your app to make outbound connections.

 SELinux (*http://selinuxproject.org/page/Main_Page*) stands for Security Enhanced Linux and is a Linux kernel module used to provide a much more secure operating system (OS). You define rules that you want to enforce, such as what processes a user can see or, in this case, which ports a user can bind to. A separate part of the kernel then enforces the rules. Using it properly can produce an incredibly secure OS; misconfigure it and you may have a barely usable system.

SELinux uses a whitelist policy for allowable ports, meaning everything is denied except for explicitly permitted ports. Fortunately, SELinux deals with labels (such as smtp_port) rather than port numbers, so OpenShift operators are able to use, for example, generic_port, which then opens quite a few ports.

At the time of writing, the SELinux policy on OpenShift Online allowed the following named SELinux labels for outbound connections:

```
mssql_port
mysqld_port
postgresql_port
git_port
oracle_port
flash_port
http_port
ftp_port
virt_migration_port
ssh_port
jacorb_port
jboss_management_port
jboss_debug_port
jboss_messaging_port
memcache_port
http_cache_port
amqp_port
generic_port
mongod_port
```

```
munin_port
pop_port
pulseaudio_port
smtp_port
whois_port
jabber_client_port
ircd_port
soundd_port
pki_ca_port
pki_ra_port
commplex_port
```

If you ever want to test if a port is available for an outbound connection, you can use the telnet command. We will combine it with the timeout command so we are not stuck if it connects to a service and we don't know how to exit out of the session. We are going to use timeout with the following syntax:

```
$ timeout -s 9 1 command
```

This tells timeout to run the following command for up to one second and then run kill 9 on the command if it hasn't returned back to the console.

Here is an example of running the full command we want over some common ports:

```
[insultapp-osbeginnerbook.rhcloud.com 6e7672676e61676976757570]\> timeout -s
9 1 telnet 127.0.0.1 6667
Trying 127.0.0.1...
telnet: connect to address 127.0.0.1: Connection refused
[insultapp-osbeginnerbook.rhcloud.com 6e7672676e61676976757570]\> timeout -s
9 1 telnet 127.0.0.1 10
Trying 127.0.0.1...
telnet: connect to address 127.0.0.1: Permission denied
[insultapp-osbeginnerbook.rhcloud.com 6e7672676e61676976757570]\> timeout -s
9 1 telnet 127.0.0.1 80
Trying 127.0.0.1...
Connected to 127.0.0.1.
Escape character is '^]'.
Killed
```

The first command is trying to connect to the localhost IP, which is different from the IP of our gear, over port 6667 (commonly used for IRC). At the end it says "Connection refused," which means the outbound connection was allowed but the server didn't accept the connection. This means on OpenShift Online you can go out over port 6667. The next attempt tries to go out over port 10 and gets a "Permission denied" error, which indicates you cannot go out on port 10. Finally, we try to go out on port 80; it is allowed, and we connect to something running that accepts the connection. After one second the Telnet process is killed by timeout.

Running this command too many times in quick succession is sure to get your application flagged and shut down by OpenShift's security scripts. Users are protected from developers who put in port-scanning applications trying to hack other people's applications. These commands are a manual means of port scanning, so if you use them too often, OpenShift will think your application has been hacked. Don't be naughty.

In the end you can see that while OpenShift restricts some of the networking functionality to protect your application and other users, there is still quite a bit you can do with the network on the platform. Most of the functionality allowed either lets you add new capabilities to your application or enhance your development experience.

## CHAPTER 8

Disk Usage

Almost all applications want to either read or store files directly on the servers they are hosted upon. These files could be images, text files, documents, or the files that the database uses to store the data. Sometimes you (or your application) just need a temporary space to output a file or store a file before processing. When you move to "the cloud," file storage has different properties than storing files on your laptop or even your own server in a rack. OpenShift has ways of handling all these application needs.

Where You Can Write "to Disk"

As an OpenShift application developer, you are given specific locations on "disk" where you are allowed to create or modify files and directories. We use disk in quotes because, as a developer, you are not actually sure what the space is located on—it could be disk drives, solid state drives, a network-attached storage (NAS) device, or any other storage location. As a developer, there are only two locations you should write files: */tmp* and the gear's *data* directory.

As on all Linux systems, you have read, write, and execute permissions for the */tmp* directory. However, unlike a typical Linux machine, where everyone on the machine shares those permissions on */tmp*, OpenShift uses pluggable authentication module (PAM) namespaces to give you your very own */tmp*. This means nobody else on the machine can see or use the */tmp* that you use. The problem with putting files here is that the space is ephemeral, meaning there is no guarantee how long a file or directory will remain there. Furthermore, any data in */tmp* will not survive an application restart.

The other directory available to you is the OpenShift data directory, which is currently at *$OPENSHIFT_HOMEDIR/app-root/data*. We use the environment variable OPEN SHIFT_DATA_DIR to point to this location. By using the environment variable you increase the portability and maintainability of your application, so we highly recommend using it in your code and configuration (see Chapter 5 for more on environment variables). In this private data directory, you also have full read, write, and execute permissions. However, this directory is persistent, allowing it to survive application stops and starts.

The data directory is where your application should store its files and put configuration settings, download themes, or generally anything you want to survive restarts and Git pushes. You can't store anything in your Git directory unless you use the Git tools. Anything written there outside of the Git lifecycle will be overwritten on the next Git push.

To clarify, the *you* we have been talking about here is actually the user ID of your application, which is a 24-character hexadecimal number. The permissions are granted to this user ID, which is the same user you identify yourself as when you SSH into or use secure FTP (SFTP) with the gear. It is also the user who owns the processes for your application servers, databases, or any other binaries you execute on the gear.

 A current limitation in OpenShift is that the data directory is not on a shared disk space for all the gears in a scalable application. This means that when a new gear spins up in a scalable application, its data directory will be empty. There is also no default method to automatically synchronize the contents of the data directories. As this book goes to print, the preferred solution for shared storage is to either use a database to store the shared entities or place them in external storage, such as Amazon's S3. We discuss the use of an external service at the end of the chapter.

Determining How Much Disk Space Is Used

At the time of writing, each gear in the OpenShift free plan was given 1 GB of disk space. If you moved into the paid tier, your gear could be up to 6 GB. The locations that count against that quota are:

- Your gear's */data directory*
- */tmp*
- Your Git repository on the gear
- The log files for your application and database servers
- The data files for your database server

The easiest way to check your disk usage is by using the RHC command-line tools:

```
rhc app show appname --gears quota
```

If you are executing the command from within the Git repository for your application, then you can omit the ``appname`` from the command. This will give you output that shows one line per gear in your application.

Here is an example:

```
Gear                     Cartridges               Used Limit
----------------------   ----------------------   ------ -----
6861736b656c6c72756c6573 postgresql-9.2              75 MB  1 GB
6c616d6264617533465766572 jbossews-2.0 haproxy-1.4 363 MB 1 GB
```

Here you can see we have two gears in this application. The gear with PostgreSQL on it is using 75 MB and the gear with JBoss is using 363 MB.

If you want to see how much disk space is used and you are comfortable with the Linux quota command, you can always SSH into a gear and use it to check your space.

To see all your gears and their SSH URLs, you can execute the command rhc app show *appname* --gears and then SSH into each gear to run quota.

OpenShift will also start to warn you both on git push and when you SSH into your gears if you exceed 90% of your quota.

 If you are not familiar with *nix-style terminal commands, especially if you are a Microsoft Windows user, please see Appendix A.

Copying Files to or from Your Local Machine

Since OpenShift uses SSH for all communication with the server, the two main ways to transfer files up to your gears are SFTP (secure FTP) and SCP (secure copy). SCP is only for moving files back and forth, while SFTP lets you do things like listing directories and removing files. You can also use any tool that can use SSH, such as rsync, but we are just going to cover SFTP and SCP here.

For people who prefer using a GUI for their file transfers, we highly recommend FileZilla, a FOSS file transfer tool that can communicate over SFTP. Please be aware, though, that FileZilla uses PuTTY-based SSH keys while OpenShift uses OpenSSH keys. You will need to convert your public SSH key to a PuTTY public key. There is a blog post (*http://bit.ly/1dK0eQs*) on the OpenShift website covering the details on how to convert your key and use FileZilla.

The syntax for using scp to copy to your gear is fairly straightforward:

```
$scp localFile 6e7672676e61676976757570@insultapp-osbeginnerbook.rhcloud.
com:/app-root/data/
```

The file localFile can also be replaced with a directory, and you can use -r to copy directories recursively. Please remember that due to file permissions, you can't write to your home directory and instead need to write to *$OPENSHIFT_DATA_DIR* or */tmp*.

The syntax to copy a file down to your machine is just as straightforward:

```
$ scp 6e7672676e61676976757570@insultapp-osbeginnerbook.rhcloud.
com:/tmp/dbbackup.tgz /data/databaseBackups/
```

Finally, you can also move files between two gears in the same application:

```
# Assumes you are in the /tmp directory on a gear
$ scp dbBackup.tgz 6e7672676e61676976757570@6e7672676e61676976757570-
osbeginnerbook.rhcloud.com:/tmp
```

Other Storage Options

The final way to create storage space for your OpenShift application is to use an external storage service such as S3 or Dropbox. You can utilize these services using the same processes as you would on your local machine—you can access them programmatically but not directly as a backup service. You could also create a Cron job (see "Writing a Cron Script" on page 73) to copy contents from your gears to one of these services.

> If there is a specific application you want to use on OpenShift, such as WordPress, we recommend doing a search for an S3 or Dropbox plug-in, such as wp-tantan-3 (*https://github.com/bradt/wp-tantan-s3*) or Updraft (*http://wordpress.org/plugins/updraftplus/*).

No matter how you look at it, there are a lot of different options for storage on OpenShift, including putting assets in your database.

## CHAPTER 9

Backup

As discussed in Chapter 8, storage space on OpenShift gears is subject to a quota. Over time, your application may well generate more data than you have space for on the platform. When you manipulate data on your gears, there is the possibility of accidental data corruption or deletion. When you deploy a new version of your application code, there is a chance, there are pesky bugs lurking between your test cases. In order to be able to respond promptly to any application issues and protect your app against unexpected data loss, you should have a backup strategy. In this chapter, we will showcase the application backup tools included in RHC and demonstrate how to use Cron to back up your database or files.

Managing Deployments and Rollbacks

When you create a new OpenShift application, it is configured out of the box to automatically deploy any changes pushed to the application Git repository. By default, only the latest version of your code is kept on your OpenShift gear. Both of these behaviors can be altered to give you more control over your deployments.

Manual Deployments

To disable the automatic deployment of pushed Git commits, use the command `rhc app-configure --no-auto-deploy`. You can change back to automatic deployment with `rhc app-configure --auto-deploy`. To deploy the latest version of the Git repository manually, use the command `rhc app deploy` *ref*. This command accepts the flags `--hot-deploy`, `--no-hot-deploy`, `--force-clean-build`, and `--no-force-clean-build`, which you can use as an alternative to or override for marker files to trigger or disable these actions (see "Using Marker Files" on page 45 for more on marker files).

Here is an example of manually deploying a new commit to Insult App:

```
[me@localhost ~/insultapp]$ rhc app-configure --no-auto-deploy
Configuring application 'insultapp' ... done

insultapp @ http://insultapp-osbeginnerbook.rhcloud.com/
(uuid: 6e7672676e61676976757570)
-------------------------------------------------------------------
    Deployment:        manual (use 'rhc deploy')
    Keep Deployments:  1
    Deployment Type:   git
    Deployment Branch: master

Your application 'insultapp' is now configured as listed above.

Use 'rhc show-app insultapp --configuration' to check your configuration values
any time.
[me@localhost ~/insultapp]$ git status
# On branch master
# Your branch is ahead of 'origin/master' by 1 commit.
#   (use "git push" to publish your local commits)
#
nothing to commit, working directory clean
[me@localhost ~/insultapp]$ git push
Counting objects: 5, done.
Delta compression using up to 4 threads.
Compressing objects: 100% (3/3), done.
Writing objects: 100% (3/3), 290 bytes | 0 bytes/s, done.
Total 3 (delta 2), reused 0 (delta 0)
To ssh://6e7672676e61676976757570@insultapp-osbeginnerbook.rhcloud.com/~/git/
insultapp.git/
   a38c5e3..c100ed9 master -> master
[me@localhost ~/insultapp]$ rhc app deploy c100ed9
Deployment of git ref 'c100ed9' in progress for application insultapp ...
```

The reference supplied as an argument to rhc app deploy can be the identifier for a
git commit, tag, or branch. In this case, we have just used the latest git commit, as
shown in the git push command output.

> We have shown deployments with Git, but it is also possible to de-
> ploy binaries with RHC. To switch to binary deployment, use the
> command rhc app-configure --deployment-type binary. You can
> then save a snapshot of your active deployment, as detailed in "Ap-
> plication Snapshots with RHC" on page 71, and deploy an altered
> version with rhc deploy /path/to/app.tar.gz -a appname.

Keeping and Utilizing Deployment History

Another feature you may wish to configure in RHC is the number of saved deployments.
By default, this is set to one, which means only the current deployment is stored. Setting
this to a higher figure will tell OpenShift to keep a copy of the application repository

and dependencies used for each recent deployment, up to the given number of deployments. This enables you to use RHC to quickly roll back to a previous deployment if something goes wrong, without having to fiddle with your Git history. The deployment files are stored in the *app-deployments* directory on the gear. They do contribute to your storage quota, so you probably do not want to keep any more history than you really need.

To configure the number of deployments stored, use the command `rhc app-configure --keep-deployments` *number*. You can list the saved deployments with `rhc deployment list` and show more information on a given one with `rhc deployment show` *id*. To activate a particular deployment, use the command `rhc deployment activate` *id*.

Here is an example of configuring the Insult App to keep the current and previous two deployments:

```
[me@localhost ~/insultapp]$ rhc app-configure --keep-deployments 3
Configuring application 'insultapp' ... done

insultapp @ http://insultapp-osbeginnerbook.rhcloud.com/
(uuid: 6e7672676e61676976757570)
-------------------------------------------------------------------
  Deployment:        auto (on git push)
  Keep Deployments:  3
  Deployment Type:   git
  Deployment Branch: master

Your application 'insultapp' is now configured as listed above.

Use 'rhc show-app insultapp --configuration' to check your configuration values
any time.
```

When we deploy our next commit, we might find we accidentally included something undesirable in our newly deployed code. We know the previously deployed version was OK, though, so we can fix that in a jiffy:

```
[me@localhost ~/insultapp]$ deployment list
3:14 PM, deployment 70692b2b
6:28 PM, deployment 7461752d
[me@localhost ~/insultapp]$ rhc deployment activate 70692b2b
Activating deployment '70692b2b' on application insultapp ...
```

Once this command completes, the application code and dependencies will be as they were before the most recent deployment.

Application Snapshots with RHC

While it is useful to be able to keep a record of your OpenShift deployments with RHC, this mechanism only keeps track of repository code and its dependencies. If you wish to take a snapshot of the entire application and its state, you should use the `rhc snap` shot command. This command exports the current state of your application, including the repository code, SQL dumps of any database cartridges, *$OPENSHIFT_DATA_DIR* files, and anything else the cartridges used are configured to export. The gzipped TAR file created can be used to later restore the state of the application.

 Both taking application snapshots and restoring an application to a saved state require the application to be stopped and restarted.

To take a snapshot of your application, use the command `rhc snapshot save`. You can add the `--filepath` *path* option to specify the location and filename of the archive file. Add the `--deployment` option if you wish to save the snapshot as a deployable file suitable for use with the `rhc deploy` command. To restore the application from the archive file, use the command `rhc snapshot restore --filepath /path/to/ tarball`. Note that not everything included in the archive is necessarily re-created; log files are not restored.

Here is an example of saving our Insult App application:

```
[me@localhost ~/insultapp]$ rhc snapshot save
Pulling down a snapshot to insultapp.tar.gz...
Creating and sending tar.gz

RESULT:
Success
[me@localhost ~/insultapp]$ ls
app.py.disabled  data  import.sql  insultapp.tar.gz  libs  README.md  setup.py
setup.pyc  setup.pyo  wsgi
```

The command produced a tarball called *insultapp.tar.gz*. Now we can make some changes, pushing a new commit and connecting to the application via SSH to delete files from the persistent data directory and add content to the database. We then decide we want to restore the previous state, which we accomplish as shown here:

```
[me@localhost ~/insultapp]$ rhc snapshot restore
Restoring from snapshot insultapp.tar.gz...
Removing old git repo: ~/git/insultapp.git/
Removing old data dir: ~/app-root/data/*
Restoring ~/git/insultapp.git and ~/app-root/data
Activation status: success

RESULT:
Success
```

The Git repository, database, and data directory are now as they were when we took the snapshot.

You can also use the `rhc snapshot` command to create a clone of an OpenShift application. To do this, create a new application of the same type (scalable/nonscalable) with the same cartridges and run the `restore` command, supplying the location of the archive file.

Backing Up Your Database

In addition to keeping deployment history and taking application snapshots with RHC, you may well want to make backups of your database. These do not require application downtime and can be performed regularly with the aid of the Cron utility. We discussed how to connect to your database using SSH in Chapter 5 and showed how to use port forwarding to interact with your database in Chapter 7. We demonstrated how to add the Cron cartridge to your application in "Cron" on page 27. In this section, we will give an example of a Cron script to create regular data dumps on the database gear and then show two approaches to moving those backups off the gear. You could write similar Cron scripts to back up other files, such as anything your application persists in *$OPENSHIFT_DATA_DIR*.

Writing a Cron Script

Our Insult App demo application uses a PostgreSQL database, so the command we will use to create SQL dumps is `pg_dump`. We want to create a backup every day, so we create the following file in our Git repository at *.openshift/cron/daily/backupdb* (if you need a refresher on OpenShift environment variables, see Chapter 5):

```
#!/bin/bash

DATE=`date +"%Y-%m-%d"`
FILE="$OPENSHIFT_APP_NAME-$DATE.sql.gz"
INIT_PATH=$OPENSHIFT_DATA_DIR/$FILE
BACKUP_DIR=$OPENSHIFT_DATA_DIR/sqlbackup

if [ ! -d "$BACKUP_DIR" ]; then
  mkdir $BACKUP_DIR
fi
pg_dump $OPENSHIFT_APP_NAME | gzip > $INIT_PATH
mv $INIT_PATH $BACKUP_DIR/$FILE
```

This Cron job will create a SQL dump every day in the persistent data directory on our gear. We have chosen to create the file in one directory and then move it to another when the SQL dump is completed to avoid any issues with partially created files when copying the backups elsewhere. To use the SQL dump to re-create the database from scratch, we could issue commands such as the following in an SSH session on the database gear:

```
[insultapp-osbeginnerbook.rhcloud.com 6e7672676e61676976757570]\> dropdb
$OPENSHIFT_APP_NAME
```

```
[insultapp-osbeginnerbook.rhcloud.com 6e7672676e61676976757570]\> createdb
$OPENSHIFT_APP_NAME
[insultapp-osbeginnerbook.rhcloud.com 6e7672676e61676976757570]\> gunzip -c
$OPENSHIFT_DATA_DIR/insultapp-sqlbackup-2014-03-14.gz | psql $OPENSHIFT_APP_NAME
```

We could also simply use the final command to run the SQL from *insultapp-sqlbackup-2014-03-14.gz* on the existing database.

 If we were creating a similar Cron job for a scalable application it would run on every gear in the app, so we would want to add logic to check which gear the commands were being executed on before attempting the SQL dump. We could use environment variables such as `OPENSHIFT_GEAR_UUID` to determine this, or check for a particular file on the target gear.

Moving Data off the Gear

In the previous section we created a Cron job to create daily database backups on our OpenShift application gear. You may also want to move or copy these backups to another location, to save storage space or in case something goes wrong with the gear. There are two approaches we can take to shifting the files: push-based or pull-based. The approach you choose will depend on your systems and situation.

If you decide to take a pull-based approach, you could create a Cron job on the system to which you want to copy the backups. This script would connect to the OpenShift gear at regular intervals and copy the backup files; one way to accomplish this would be using the `rsync` tool. Here is an example of a pull-based daily Cron script for Insult App:

```
#!/bin/bash
rsync -avz --remove-source-files -e ssh 6e7672676e61676976757570@insultapp-
osbeginnerbook.rhcloud.com:~/app-root/data/sqlbackup /backup
```

This job copies the *sqlbackup* directory and its files from the gear to the local directory at */backup*. It also deletes the files from the gear after they have been successfully copied. For this to work, the system running the job must be able to access the OpenShift gear via SSH; its public key should have been added to the related OpenShift account (see Chapter 5 for more on accessing gears via SSH).

The second alternative is a push-based approach. You may wish to push files to an external service such as Amazon S3 or Dropbox, or your own server. In order to use SSH and associated tools such as `scp` or `rsync` to send files from your gear to elsewhere, you will need access to a public/private key pair on the gear. The *.ssh* directory within an OpenShift user's home directory is not writable, so we will need to create a new key set within the persistent *data* directory. You can do so by issuing the following commands on your gear. In this example, we do not set a passphrase for the key pair; if you wish to set a passphrase you will need to modify the Cron script shown to deal with this:

```
[insultapp-osbeginnerbook.rhcloud.com 6e7672676e616769767575570]\> mkdir
$OPENSHIFT_DATA_DIR/.ssh
[insultapp-osbeginnerbook.rhcloud.com 6e7672676e616769767575570]\> ssh-keygen -f
$OPENSHIFT_DATA_DIR/.ssh/id_rsa
Generating public/private rsa key pair.
Enter passphrase (empty for no passphrase):
Enter same passphrase again:
Your identification has been saved in ...openshift/var/lib/openshift/
6e7672676e616769767575570/app-root/data//.ssh/id_rsa.
Your public key has been saved in /var/lib/openshift/6e7672676e616769767575570/
app-root/data//.ssh/id_rsa.pub.
The key fingerprint is:
4e:79:61:6e:79:61:6e:79:61:6e:79:61:6e:79:61:21 6e7672676e616769767575570@ex-std-
node710.prod.rhcloud.com
The key's randomart image is:
+--[ RSA 2048]----+
|           . ==@|
|            *oXo|
|           +.+.=|
|          +...  |
|         S = +  |
|          + .   |
|          E     |
|                |
|                |
+----------------+
[insultapp-osbeginnerbook.rhcloud.com 6e7672676e616769767575570]\> ls
$OPENSHIFT_DATA_DIR/.ssh
id_rsa  id_rsa.pub
```

This command has created two files for us: the private SSH key contained in *id_rsa* and the public key in *id_rsa.pub*. We will need to add *id_rsa.pub* to the SSH configuration for the target *user* on our backup server, which we are going to call *mybackupserver.com* because we are breathtakingly original. One way to do this would be copying the entire contents of the new *id_rsa.pub* file and adding it to *~/.ssh/authorized_hosts* in *user*'s home directory on the target server.

Now that we have access to a private SSH key on the gear, here is a revised version of the Insult App *.openshift/cron/daily/backupdb* script from the previous section that both creates the SQL dump and copies it to another server using the scp (secure copy) command:

```
#!/bin/bash

DATE=`date +"%Y-%m-%d"`
FILEPATH="$OPENSHIFT_DATA_DIR/$OPENSHIFT_APP_NAME-$DATE.sql.gz"

pg_dump $OPENSHIFT_APP_NAME | gzip > $FILEPATH
```

```
scp -i $OPENSHIFT_DATA_DIR/.ssh/id_rsa -o StrictHostKeyChecking=no $FILEPATH
user@mybackupserver.com:~/backup && rm $FILEPATH
```

This script creates the SQL dump in the persistent data directory on the OpenShift gear, copies the archive to *backup* within *user*'s home directory on *mybackupserver.com* (the *backup* directory should already exist), and, if this action is successful, deletes the file on the gear. The secure copy command references the private SSH key we created on the OpenShift gear with the -i (identity file) option. We have disabled StrictHostKey Checking as we do not want the Cron job to wait for someone to type "yes" to approve the connection; we want to be off doing something way more entertaining while our backup script works its magic each day.

In this chapter, we have shown three different ways to keep backup copies of aspects of your OpenShift application: deployment history, snapshots, and database dumps. We have also discussed how to do manual and binary deployments on the platform and how to move files from OpenShift to elsewhere. The way that you utilize these techniques to form your application backup strategy is dependent on your individual needs, so we cannot prescribe a one-size-fits-all approach. However, at a minimum we would recommend that you back up your database periodically, as well as any files persisted elsewhere. Carefully consider the impact of any data loss or downtime when deciding how frequently your backups should be performed and how much deployment history to store.

## CHAPTER 10

Team Collaboration

In our discussion so far we have generally considered OpenShift and its features from the point of view of a single developer. However, whether you embrace Agile, post-Agile Programmer Anarchy, or some other newfangled way of working, most of us develop software in teams. In this chapter, we will broaden our scope beyond the lone wolf and look at OpenShift's offerings for the whole wolf pack. We will show how to manage multiple SSH keys and how to use an OpenShift domain to collaborate, before concluding with some thoughts about possible platform workflows.

Managing Multiple SSH Keys

One way of enabling another person to make changes to your OpenShift application code is to add her machine's public SSH key to your OpenShift account. This will enable your collaborator to access the Git repositories of any of your OpenShift applications using standard Git commands. It will not grant that person access to your OpenShift Online account, or enable her to log in to RHC.

This method for code sharing is best suited to situations where the person you wish to grant access to does not have an OpenShift account. If she's willing to create an OpenShift account or has one already, a better way to give access is to add her to your application's domain, as explained in the next section.

You can manage the SSH keys for your OpenShift account from the command line with the `rhc sshkey` command. You can list all your SSH keys with `rhc sshkey list`, add a key with `rhc sshkey add`, and remove a key with `rhc sshkey remove`. To add your collaborator, have her supply you with her public SSH key; typically, this would be her *~/.ssh/id_rsa.pub* file (this is the public part of the key pair; the corresponding private key file, *id_rsa*, should never be shared). Here is an example of adding a new key to an OpenShift account:

```
[me@localhost ~]$ rhc sshkey add myfriend ~/Downloads/id_rsa.pub
RESULT:
SSH key id_rsa.pub has been added as 'myfriend'
```

Once the key has been added, give your collaborator the Git URL of the OpenShift application repository you want her to edit (you can view this with `rhc apps`). She can use this URL with the regular `git clone` command, and will also be able to access the application gear via `ssh`. If you want to add more collaborators, simply add more SSH keys.

Domain Access for Teams

Adding SSH keys to your OpenShift account is one way of enabling collaboration on application code, but it has limitations; it will not allow your team members to use RHC commands with the shared apps, and it gives everyone you add full access to make changes. A more flexible approach is to add members to your OpenShift domain.

All OpenShift applications must belong to a domain, sometimes referred to as a namespace. This becomes part of the OpenShift Online application URL, which has the form **appname-domain**.*rhcloud.com*—this should look familiar by now. Depending on your OpenShift account, you may be able to create multiple domains; users on the free tier of OpenShift Online are limited to one domain.

OpenShift domains can be managed from the command line with the `rhc domain` command. Use `rhc domain list` to see which domains you have access to and `rhc domain show` to display the details of applications in a domain. If you have access to do so, you can create new domains with `rhc domain create` *name*.

Domain membership can also be managed from the command line, using the `rhc mem ber` command. When you add a member to a domain, you can give that member one of three possible roles:

view

> Viewers can see information about the domain and its applications but cannot make any changes. They cannot use `rhc env` to view environment variables, access the application via SSH, or clone the Git repository (unless their SSH public keys have also been added to the domain OpenShift account).

edit

> Editors can do everything viewers can do, plus create, update, and delete applications in the domain. They can view and edit environment variables and access application Git repositories and gears via SSH.

admin

> Administrators can do everything editors can do, as well as update domain membership and change the domain name.

These member permissions apply to all applications within a domain. If you wish to give the same user a different level of access to different applications, you should place them in separate domains.

Here is an example of adding and then removing a member in Insult App's domain, *osbeginnerbook*. OpenShift users are referenced by their username, which is usually their email address; rhc account will display the details of the logged-in user:

```
[me@localhost ~]$ rhc member add phb@redhat.com -n osbeginnerbook --role view
Adding 1 viewer to domain ... done
[me@localhost ~]$ rhc member list -n osbeginnerbook
Login                   Role
----------------------- -------------
TheSteve0@redhat.com    admin (owner)
codemiller@redhat.com   admin
phb@redhat.com          view
[me@localhost ~]$ rhc member remove phb@redhat.com -n osbeginnerbook
Removing 1 member from domain ... done
```

A domain member can use the command rhc domain leave -n *domain* if she wishes to remove herself from a domain.

Possible Workflows

If you have read to this point, you should now have a good idea of how the OpenShift platform works and what features it offers. However, you may still be wondering how to adapt your current team processes to use OpenShift. Every team is different, so we cannot offer a magic formula for this, but here are some points you may want to consider:

- User access is restricted at the domain level on OpenShift, as discussed earlier. Given this, you will probably want to create a domain for each of your environments (development, integration, test, stage, production, etc.) and add those who should have access as members with the appropriate role (view, edit, admin).
- No one likes accidental production deployments. Consider turning off auto-deploy for all apps in your production domain (see "Manual Deployments" on page 69).
- Think about restricting pushes to the staging or production environments to your ops users.

Taking into account these items, here are the details of a possible team workflow utilizing OpenShift:

1. Create a new Git repository for your project. This is the upstream for all development. This repository should not contain anything related to OpenShift, such as the *.openshift* directory.

2. Create an integration domain for the team. Add all the team members and give them edit rights using the `rhc member add` command. This will be used as an integration environment. Create an OpenShift application for the app under development in the integration domain. This application should probably be scalable, to match the corresponding production application.

3. Create a domain for each developer where developers can create their own versions of the application and try out changes before they push them to the integration domain.

4. To push changes to the development or integration environments, the developers use Git remotes. This means when a developer issues the command `git push dev master`, his changes are deployed to the development environment. After testing, he can do a `git push int master` to push the changes to the integration environment.

5. The integration environment has the Jenkins cartridge (or an alternative continuous integration cartridge) installed to build the project and run all the test cases. When team members push their code to this domain, it automatically builds and tests the application and will not deploy it if the tests do not pass. If there are other environments in the pipeline, such as a QA environment, they may also have continuous integration set up to do other levels of testing, such as functional or user acceptance testing.

6. Create staging and production domains containing OpenShift applications with the same cartridges as the app under development; only grant rights to the operations team members, or whoever should have the right to push deployments to prod. After the testers have inspected the quality of the application in the integration domain, they push the latest version to staging using the command `git push staging master`. When it comes time to do a deployment, the ops people can then tag the release and push it to production with `git push production master`. Only the ops people should have admin rights for the production domain.

7. The new version of the application is now in production, but it has not yet been deployed as it is configured with RHC for manual deployment. When deployment is scheduled, the ops person uses the `rhc deploy` command to manually deploy the application.

This workflow is not going to suit everyone and does not cover all aspects of the development process, but we hope it sparks some ideas of how OpenShift could become part of your team.

CHAPTER 11
Summary

Now, sadly, it is time to wrap up the book. We hope it has been as much fun to read as it was to write. Most importantly, we hope our book fulfilled its purpose: to get you up and running comfortably with OpenShift as fast as possible.

What We Covered

To quickly recap, we covered:

- Some basic terminology explaining the OpenShift components
- How to create an application on OpenShift
- How to modify the template application to use your own code
- How to add other functionality to your application, such as a database or Cron job
- How to use the command line with your application to interact with the database
- How to use environment variables to add other functionality to your application
- How to work with your log files and create new ones if needed
- How to add external library dependencies to your application
- How to add WebSocket functionality to your application
- What networking options are available and what external ports you can use
- Where you can write to disk in your OpenShift application
- How to manage your disk space
- How to back up your database
- How to back up your entire application
- How to use OpenShift to work on a team project

That is a lot of territory covered in a relatively short number of pages. We also used a Python application to illustrate the pattern of development on OpenShift.

Other Areas to Explore

To learn about other people using OpenShift and their projects, check out the OpenShift Developer Spotlight (*http://bit.ly/1r4Y46J*). The OpenShift team also loves to show off the great applications built by users in the Application Gallery (*http://bit.ly/1hNgx1k*). Now that we have taught you how to do all this great stuff, we expect your cool application or biography any minute now.

If you want a more in-depth explanation of development on OpenShift, we highly recommend the OpenShift Online User Guide (*http://red.ht/1d7rU6P*). This guide is also short, but covers some different topics from our book. It is well worth a read.

While we are great authors, in the highly unlikely scenario where you might need other help than this book, there are also great resources on the OpenShift website, such as the Knowledge Base (*https://www.openshift.com/kb*) and FAQs (*https://www.open shift.com/faq*). OpenShift Online has moved to Stack Overflow (*http://bit.ly/ 1eYW33t*) for Q&A, type resources.

There is also a Developer Center (*https://www.openshift.com/developers*) on the Open-Shift site. It has information on how to use the Web Console or Eclipse IDE integration. You can also find information there on how to create your own QuickStarts (*https:// www.openshift.com/developers/get-involved/creating-quickstarts*) for your favorite applications. The site also covers how to add your own preferred server technology using a custom cartridge (*http://bit.ly/1qCuZ2o*). Most importantly, the resource center has links to other languages and databases OpenShift supports, so you can dig in to more specific material for your programming language of choice.

If you want to dive deeper into OpenShift itself, you would like to learn how to run it on your own infrastructure so you can tweak it to your liking, or you love Ruby and want to be part of an open source project, we highly recommend you visit the OpenShift Origin site (*http://openshift.github.io/*). Origin is the upstream project for the other two products and it has a friendly and active community. There are many ways to get involved in the community. Here are some links to get you started:

- All the code is up on GitHub (*https://github.com/openshift/*).
  - Pull requests from the community are welcome, and they go through the same process as Red Hatter pull requests.
  - You can also add GitHub issues.
  - There are guidelines on how to contribute (*http://bit.ly/1cYGZb5*) to the project.

- You can see the product roadmap and what the teams are working on for each sprint on the OpenShift Trello boards (*https://trello.com/openshift*).
- There is a public Bugzilla instance (*http://red.ht/1qCLRWP*).
- You can come chat in IRC on *irc.freenode.net*—application developers should come talk in *#openshift* and people interested in running OpenShift or modifying the platform should drop in to *#openshift-dev*.
- There are weekly hangouts (*http://bit.ly/1fwwJBj*) on Google+.

There are also at least two other published books on OpenShift, with several more books at various stages of writing or publication. If you are interested in running OpenShift Origin, then we recommend our colleague Adam Miller's book, *Implementing Open-Shift* (*http://bit.ly/1fwwR3F*) (Packt). For a book like ours, aimed at developers using OpenShift, but with a focus on JBoss technologies, look to our colleague Eric Schabell's book, *OpenShift Primer* (*http://bit.ly/1ilgA73*) (Developer.Press).

Final Words

Always check the OpenShift website and blog for the latest and greatest features. PaaS is a rapidly evolving area, and the OpenShift team has made a commitment to pushing the state of the art forward. The team is also committed to listening to the users—if you have suggestions for the service you can always write to Steve or Katie, or to *open shift@redhat.com*. One of the things we love about working with OpenShift is that the more you use it, the more possibilities emerge—so the most important thing at this point is for you to get coding!

Basic Linux for Non-Linux Users

In this appendix, we give a short introduction to the Linux filesystem for Windows (and Mac nonterminal) users. You will need this information because your application will be hosted on a Linux machine (Red Hat Enterprise Linux, in particular). One shortcut you should know right away is that the tilde character (~) is an alias for your home directory. The operating system will expand that symbol to the path to your home directory.

Listing Directory Contents

To list the contents of a folder, you can execute the `ls` command. This will show the contents of the directory, but will not display any information about permissions or which items are directories. To view the permissions for items, use the command `ls -l`. Use `ls -lh` for human-readable file sizes, or `ls -lha` to list all files, including hidden files. The output should look something like this:

```
[me@localhost tmp]$ ls -lha
total 92K
drwxrwxr-x.  3 me me 4.0K Jun 28 06:28 .
drwx------. 58 me me 4.0K Jun 28 03:14 ..
drwxrwxr-x.  2 me me 4.0K Jun 28 06:28 a_directory
-rw-rw-r--.  1 me me  78K Jun 28 06:28 example.txt
```

Reading from left to right, the first 11 characters represent the file type and permissions. If the first character is a *d*, it means the line refers to a directory. The next three characters are the permissions for the user, the following three are the permissions for the group, and the next three are the permissions for the "world." Each character represents a differently capability: *r* stands for read, *w* stands for write, and *x* stands for execute. For example, the file *example.txt* has read and write permissions for the owner and group but only read permissions for the world. If there were a shell script in this file you would not be able to execute the script because the execute permission is not set. The final . in the 11 characters indicates that extended attributes are enabled; in this case it is SELinux permissions.

The next field, always a number, gives the number of directories and files that are linked from that resource. For example, *a_directory* contains two "things" inside it: the first is a reference to the directory above it and the second is the directory itself.

The next item is the owner of the resource, in this case the user *me*, followed by the Linux group for that resource, which in this case is also *me*. They do not have to be the same value.

Following that is the size of the resource and then the date and time of last modification. Finally, we have the name of the resource. By default, anything that starts with a dot (.) is not output when you use the `ls` or `ls -l` commands. For example *.myHiddenDirectory* would not show up. Again, to get `ls` to show the hidden files you need to use the `-a` flag.

There are two special resources that will always show up when executing `ls -la`: the . and .. resources. The single dot (.) refers to the current directory, which is good to know from a permissions perspective, and the double dot (..) is the directory above.

To change to the parent directory, you can use the command `cd ...` If you want to execute a file in a certain directory you have to first make sure the execute bit is set (which we will show you how to change soon) and second, preface the command with a `./`. So, for example, the way to execute a script would be `./myScript.sh`. Hopefully you now see how the . and .. are expanded in those two commands.

Changing Permissions

To change permissions on a file or directory, you use the `chmod` command. As with most Linux commands, you can use `chmod --help` to get a brief help output and use `man chmod` to get a more detailed explanation. We are going to show you the basic syntax, which looks like `chmod who action permission resource` where:

- `who` is:
  - `u` = user
  - `g` = group
  - `o` = world
  - `a` = all three of these groups (`ugo`)
- `action` is:
  - `+` = add the permission
  - `-` = remove the permission

— = = whatever permission specified; overwrites the previous permissions

- `permission` is (we are only listing the most common):
  - r = read
  - w = write
  - x = execute

For example, if we wanted to change the execute settings on *example.txt* for the owner we would do this at the command prompt: **`chmod u+x example.txt`**. If we wanted to change the permissions on all the contents of *a_directory* and any subdirectories to maximum permissiveness, we would do **`chmod -R a+rwx a_directory`**; the -R option is to apply the permissions recursively. Be careful with using -R—with great power comes great responsibility.

Working with Files and Directories

In Linux, you can carry out various operations on files and directories from the command line.

Creating Files

You can create files by opening the new **`filename`** in your text editor. For example, Steve likes Nano as a text editor (nice and simple), so he would just do `nano myNew File.txt`. Katie prefers Vim, so she would use the command `vim myNewFile.txt`. If you wanted to create an empty file, you could use `touch`. If you execute the command `touch myNewFile.txt`, it will create the new empty file. You can also use `touch` to update the last modified time of an existing file to the time when you execute the command.

Moving Files and Directories

Moving files is achieved with the command `mv`. The syntax is pretty simple: `mv` **`old/dir/ filename.txt new/dir/newfilename.txt`**. This command is also commonly used to rename files by moving the file to a new name in the same directory: `mv oldFile Name.txt newFileName.txt`.

Copying Files and Directories

The command for copying files and directories is `cp`. As with the `chmod` commands, you can also use it recursively with the -R flag. Here is the syntax for the command: `cp` **`file.txt directory/toCopyTo/`**.

Deleting Files

Deleting a file is also very simple. It is accomplished with the command `rm`. To remove a file *filename.txt,* you could execute the command `rm filename.txt`. As with changing permissions, you can execute deletion recursively; however, you should use this with extreme caution as there is no undo button. For example, to remove all text files from the current directory downward, you could do `rm -r *.txt`.

You can also use this command to remove a directory and all its contents at the same time: `rm -r myDirectory/`. Did we mention you should use this carefully?

If you are prompted to confirm each deletion and you feel confident you are correct, you can use the `-f` flag to tell `rm` to force the removal.

Creating Directories

Directories are created with the `mkdir` command: `mkdir myNewDir`.

Deleting Directories

The safe way to remove a directory is to:

1. Remove all the files in the directory.
2. Remove the directory using the `rmdir` command: `rmdir myEmptyDir`.

As mentioned before, you can use `rm` to do the same thing in one fell swoop, but you should do so cautiously.

Where To Learn More

There are plenty of websites that can teach you the basic Linux commands, and there is a collection of tutorials at the Linux.com tutorial site (*http://www.linux.com/learn*). We would also recommend the following books:

1. *Linux Pocket Guide, 2nd Edition* by Daniel J. Barrett (O'Reilly)
2. *The Linux Command Line: A Complete Introduction*, by William E. Shotts Jr. (No Starch Press)

If you want to have a system to practice these commands with we recommend installing the Fedora or CentOS operating system, either as a dual boot on your machine or in a virtual machine. We suggest Fedora or CentOS because they have the closest syntax to the shell on Red Hat Enterprise Linux, which is the OS underneath OpenShift Online.

About the Authors

Steven Pousty is a dad, son, partner, and PaaS Dust Spreader (aka developer evangelist) with OpenShift. He goes around and shows off all the great work the OpenShift engineers do. He can teach you about PaaS with Java, Python, PostgreSQL, MongoDB, and some JavaScript. He has deep subject area expertise in GIS/Spatial, statistics, and ecology. He has spoken at over 50 conferences and done over 30 workshops including Monktoberfest, MongoNY, JavaOne, FOSS4G, CTIA, AjaxWorld, GeoWeb, Where2.0, and OSCON. Before OpenShift, Steve was a developer evangelist for LinkedIn, deCarta, and ESRI. Steve has a PhD in Ecology from University of Connecticut. He likes building interesting applications and helping developers create great solutions.

Katie Miller, also known as codemiller, works as an OpenShift Developer Advocate at Red Hat. Katie is a polyglot programmer with a penchant for Haskell. The functional programming enthusiast cofounded the Lambda Ladies online community and co-organizes the Brisbane Functional Programming Group. Katie is a familiar face at an array of meetup groups spanning a variety of programming language communities, including Java, JavaScript, Python, and Ruby. The former newspaper journalist has presented at conferences and meetups across Australia and New Zealand, and as far afield as Budapest, Hungary. Katie is passionate about coding, open source, software quality, languages of all kinds, and encouraging more girls and women to pursue careers in technology.

Colophon

The animal on the cover of *Getting Started with OpenShift* is a purple-naped lory (*Lorius domicella*), a species of parrot in the Psittaculidae family. Endemic to the Indonesian islands of Ambon, Seram, Saparua, Haruku, and South Maluku, these vibrantly colored birds are considered a vulnerable species due to trapping for the cage-bird trade.

The purple-naped Lory, named for the way the black on top of its head fades to purple at the nape of its neck, is mostly red, with a red tail that darkens to a deeper red at the tip. Its wings are green; it has blue thighs and a yellow band across its chest. Adults have orange beaks, whereas juveniles have brown beaks and lighter, grey-white eyerings, and a wider band of yellow across the chest. The purple neck is also more extensive on juveniles than on adults. The Lory can grow up to 11 inches (28 cm) and average about 8.2 oz (235 g) in weight.

The cover image is from *Johnson's Natural History*. The cover fonts are URW Typewriter and Guardian Sans. The text font is Adobe Minion Pro; the heading font is Adobe Myriad Condensed; and the code font is Dalton Maag's Ubuntu Mono.

Milton Keynes UK
Ingram Content Group UK Ltd.
UKHW052104271124
451713UK00007B/122